"Bob Staffanson's journey from rural Montana to a prestigious conductor's podium in western Massachusetts is remarkable; the culmination of his life in decades of service to the highest ideals of human achievement, working with Native American elders, is profound. By turning his back on racism and materialism, he has given us, in *Witness to Spirit*, both wisdom and a modern example of an exemplary life."

Barry Lopez, Author of *Arctic Dreams* and *Of Wolves and Men*

"Robert Staffanson has created a story that honors his own evolution from cowboy to symphony conductor before abandoning wealth and fame to work with indigenous people and learn the ways of wisdom. This is a book that reminds us our lives are blessedly made of stories. Gratitude is the word that remains after reading *Witness to Spirit*."

Terry Tempest Williams, Author of *Refuge, When Women Were Birds*, and *The Hour of Land*

"With *Witness to Spirit*, Robert Staffanson becomes a symbol for our best chance as a culture: abandon all we've been told we deserve and embrace the native mind for its beauty and depth, but also for what it knows about saving our species over and over again."

Brooke Williams, Author of *Open Midnight*

"Profound values, insights, integrity, courage, commitment, mastery, wisdom, leadership, and humor … a complete privilege."

Annika Dopping, TV Producer, Sweden

"*Witness to Spirit* truly speaks to my heart."

Jane Riley, Life Long Learning Organization

"His tone is that of the true pioneer—more matter-of-fact than melodramatic ... Staffanson's realistic narrative shows how true, long-term commitment is needed in any human rights endeavors. *Witness to Spirit* sagely concludes that the integration of energies is key to preserving our past and preparing for a better future."
   Foreword Reviews

"Staffanson proves to be an insightful, articulate and thoughtful author. This is an important, unforgettable book full of wisdom that, once read, will leave you changed in the way you think about America, Montana, the West, native people and potential courses of action in these troubling times."
   Bozeman Magazine

"Staffanson's story is inspiring, conveying rock-solid values and a depth of feeling sufficient to propel one human being on an amazing and fulfilling trajectory."
   MassLive

"The most interesting man in Montana? Hell, he might be the most interesting man in America."
   Last Best News of Montana

"*Witness to Spirit* reads like the man himself—uncomplicated, straightforward and profound. Bob Staffanson's life work brings us all closer to our true path and serves as a reminder that we can each make a difference; in fact, we have a moral obligation to do so."
   Pamela Roberts, Rattlesnake Productions, Inc.

"What a fantastic life! Bob's work will continue for generations because of his ability to inspire others to see things differently."
   Sharyn Anhalt, Friends of the Bozeman Public Library

Witness to Spirit

My Life with Cowboys, Mozart & Indians

ROBERT STAFFANSON

Cowboy, Symphony Conductor, Founder of the American Indian Institute

Witness to Spirit:
My Life with Cowboys, Mozart & Indians

Robert Staffanson

Hardcover ISBN: 9781942545224
Library of Congress Control Number: 2015954837

Paperback ISBN: 9781942545217

Text and Photography ©2016 Robert Staffanson.
All rights reserved.

Edited by Karen Kibler.
Book design by Nancy Cleary.

No part of this book may be reproduced in any manner whatsoever without written permission except in the case of brief quotations embodied in critical articles and reviews. Publisher and editor are not liable for any typographical errors, content mistakes, inaccuracies, or omissions related to the information in this book. Product trade names or trademarks mentioned throughout this publication remain property of their respective owners.

Wyatt-MacKenzie Publishing
DEADWOOD, OREGON
www.WyattMacKenzie.com

www.WitnesstoSpirit.com

Publisher's Cataloging-in-Publication Data

Staffanson, Robert.
    Witness to spirit : my life with cowboys , Mozart & Indians / Robert Staffanson.
    pages cm
    ISBN 978-1-942545-22-4
1. Staffanson, Robert. 2. Ranch life—Biography. 3. Montana—Biography.
4. Conductors (Music)—Biography. 5. Political activists—Biography.
6. Indians of North America—Civil Rights. I. Title.

F767 .S73 2015
978.7/033092—dc23   2015954837

DEDICATION

*Dedicated to Ann,
and our family.*

TABLE OF CONTENTS

Foreword by Oren Lyons i
An Introduction by Todd Wilkinson ix

PRELUDE
Pondering the Meaning of Time 17

FIRST MOVEMENT
Cowboys 23

SECOND MOVEMENT
Music 73

THIRD MOVEMENT
Indians 151

POSTLUDE
Witness to Spirit 243

Photography Notes 250

Index 253

FOREWORD

Written by Oren Lyons

Cowboys & Indians

It all started with an invitation to attend a Leadership meeting of native and non-native people at the famous conference center in Wisconsin. The invitation centered on collaboration, but it was not clear how this could occur. Everyone arrived with their own ideas; the energy was high and there were small groups engaged in spirited discussions. There were many notable attendees from both sides, more non-native than native. I saw some of my friends with PhDs but not any traditional Indian leaders. Then I met Bob Staffanson for the first time. He was an imposing figure with a shock of greying hair. He moved with the easy grace of a man who spent a lot of time outdoors. Indeed,

as I found out, he was a cowboy from Montana. At the end of the event, he approached me and asked if I would be willing to attend a follow-up meeting. I said, although it was an interesting meeting, I didn't think I could say much to the next meeting. He asked why not and I said that I did not see traditional Indians here. He said they were who he wanted to talk with, to see if they would be willing to work with him, communicating across cultures to create better understanding, and to educate White people on their relationship to nature. I told him the leaders that I know would probably not say a word in a meeting like this. He had an interesting idea, but I knew that the spiritual leaders would not be comfortable in a setting like this.

He said, "If you can set up a meeting I'll pay for their travel and stay." I said, "If they met it would be by themselves and they would not speak if there were white people there." Bob understood that our people, our traditional and spiritual leaders, knew things which would help his people. White brothers understanding the world better would result in better behavior on their part. He wanted us to share our knowledge with them for the common good.

That was asking a lot from us. My mind went back to a recent meeting in a Hopi kiva with their elders, where the issue of non-native people asking for help and direction came up. A very old Hopi elder said there was a prophecy saying this would happen. Maybe this was the time.

I thought about our Unity Caravan made up of traditional Indian elders and people, now on its fourth year of travelling across North America advising Indian nations and people to get back to their ceremonies and traditions. This, I thought, may be the time. I said to Bob that I would ask the elders. All of this took place in the early 1970s.

I talked to my elders and they agreed that it was worth

a meeting. So in the late summer of 1977, native delegates from Hopi, Puyallup, Muskogee, Northern Cheyenne, Onondaga, Seneca, Mohawk, and Crow met at Three Forks, Montana in this now historic first assembly of what was to become The Traditional Circle of Indian Elders and Youth, supported by Bob's organization, the American Indian Institute.

In the beginning I didn't completely trust Bob. We all wanted to see what he was made of, and I must say that over the course of many years, many decades—he and I are ten years apart in age—he has become a very good friend. He is like a brother. I remember some of those first gatherings of the Circle with elders gathered around and Bob stayed at the edge, watching, listening. He stood back. For a White person to do that—to not try and insert himself in the conversation or enlarge his presence or self-importance, to be humble and modest—is really extraordinary because it has happened so seldom over centuries of interaction between Indians and the Europeans who came here.

Different tribes are now communicating with each other, in ways that didn't happen for 500 years, because of the Two Circles. And we're talking with our brothers and sisters in Africa and Asia and people in the north of Scandinavia and Russia and the South Seas. He knew we have an important perspective to offer the world. It isn't political wisdom, it rises up out of the ground. Our wisdom is based upon respect for the earth and offering thanks for enabling us to survive.

We met at Three Forks for three days and decided that the idea had merit and we would think about it and meet again next year. After the fifth year our meetings became an annual event without discussing if we would meet again next year. Our Two Circles have still not met

collectively. We said to Bob that our nations would need healing and repair before we could help our brothers.

Our Circle decided to issue an annual communication, reflecting and sharing the discussions that had taken place in our annual meetings. It would then be up to the American Indian Institute to distribute the communiques. Several years ago we decided that the communiques were not good enough and that we needed to do better. We decided to hold public forums to exchange and discuss with our non-native partners the issues and subjects of the annual meetings; that way we could get an exchange and continuing dialogue.

The first forum was hosted by the Red Lake Chippewa. Our leaders met for a sunrise ceremony as is the custom in our annual meeting. We burnt a fire to begin the ceremony and to our surprise some of the non-native participants appeared at the fire. We were uncertain how to address this; as we conferred an eagle landed on a tree close to the fire. That confirmed the ceremony and our non-native friends joined our circle.

This shared sunrise ceremony has become a part of the forum. I have lost track of the date of our first contact with Bob Staffanson but it is close to forty years that the Circle he initiated has been meeting, and it has been good for all of us.

I think Bob's legacy is that he helped native people come together in ways that we never did before. You may think that I am talking about just holding meetings and being a logistics planner. That isn't it. The essence of the Two Circles is to get Indians talking, to share our stories and to come together in spirit from across different corners of the North American continent and the rest of the world to speak with a powerful unified voice that is uniquely our

own. Some people are threatened by that. We make some people in the United States nervous. For thousands of years tribes thrived on this continent. We had our own languages, customs, and ways of life. And all this time our connections to the land, and our respect for the Creator, were pretty much identical. It didn't matter—if you were Onondaga like me, or Navajo in the Southwest, if you were Seminole in the Southeast or Athabascan—there is mutual recognition. But in our isolation, made worse by the colonization by Europeans, it left many tribes to believe we're alone as islands that were only getting smaller and smaller.

When you are alone you don't feel as if you have any friends and allies. What I respect about Bob is that as a non-indigenous person he could have ignored the abuses being carried out by his own culture. He asked, "What can I do to help?" and our response was to bring traditional elders together. He made it happen and then he got out of the way.

Ann, Bob's wife, has been a major supporter for all of us. Women are such a power in all of our lives. Krissie, his daughter, and her family have been unwavering in the love and support of our Two Circles. Bob is the leader and Chief of his circle. He is 94. The elder leader of our circle, Joe Medicine Crow, is 104. I'm the youngster here at 85. We're still here to do our best for the coming generations; there's no better work than that.

Peace to one and all.
Josequistto (Oren Lyons) Faithkeeper, Turtle Clan
Onondaga Council of Chiefs
Haudenosaunee

ROBERT STAFFANSON
AN INTRODUCTION

Written by Todd Wilkinson

No one I know—or ever met—has undergone radical reinvention the way Robert Staffanson has. But he's actually done it twice. The arc of his life involves a progression through a trio of distinct movements spread across almost a century, each interwoven and interconnected by the same moral compass, but none serving as a logical, predictable antecedent to the next. To understand what I am talking about, ponder:

* Raised on cattle ranches in rural Montana, Staffanson first identifies as a *cowboy*.

* Later, he becomes a *symphony conductor* making a name for himself in the highbrow world of temperamental, classical music maestros on the East Coast and beyond.

* In mid-life, and then spanning half a century, he emerges from a cocoon, completing a metamorphosis, emerging as … are you ready for this … a quiet, self-effacing *civil rights activist*. Wholly awakened to the struggle of American indigenous peoples—Indians—he says goodbye to his former life and joins a global fight for human rights and justice.

I've never encountered another Westerner like him.

Now that I have your full attention, as your thoughts spin just as mine did, allow me to elaborate further on the stages in Staffanson's enigmatic transformation.

As a native son of the West, he grew up on the backs of horses. He is a product of the cowboy culture of myth and lore, defined by its brawny mystique, masculine physicality, and quiet, hard-nosed stoicism that fits the stereotype most of us carry in our minds. Staffanson wore denim, leather boots with spurs on the heels, chaps on thighs; riding with hands calloused by rope, tack-adorning saddle, and yes, a sweat-stained vaquero hat brimmed just over the brow.

During his coming of age, first along the lonesome flanks of the Yellowstone River near the badlands of far eastern Montana, and subsequently in the Deer Lodge Valley girded by mountains on the western side of the state, Staffanson arguably was headed toward just another bucolic existence.

But along this journey, the rawhide man was summoned to another calling, his ear finely tuned in childhood to an ambient, open-air soundtrack playing in his head. Imprinted on his psyche were the melodies of his father's fiddle and mother's singing of prairie church hymns. From his earliest sanguine memories of childhood—in the 1920s and 1930s—Staffanson recalls a close relationship with the violin that he came to know as intimately as a lariat.

This love affair led the sensitive wrangler to attain a college degree in music at the University of Montana. Against long odds and doubts expressed by others, Staffanson founded the first symphony orchestra in Montana's largest city and, by fluke of fate, attended a national, invitation-only, conductor's workshop in Philadelphia where the great maestro Eugene Ormandy was presiding.

Totally unexpected, Ormandy took a liking to the young unassuming cowboy conductor and opened a proverbial door, seeing in him promise and spirit. Through that threshold of kismet, Staffanson landed a prestigious conducting post with a renowned regional symphony in Massachusetts. The Springfield Symphony, in fact, commanded a reputation surpassed only by the Boston Symphony.

Under his direction, Staffanson harnessed the talents of an extraordinary assemblage of classical musicians and he met legends like Aaron Copeland and Leonard Bernstein, in addition to other prominent contemporaries in Europe. The kid from the Old Wild West was, in a tuxedo and directing a baton, putting his interpretation on Old World masterworks such as Mozart's Requiem, Beethoven's 9th, and Puccini's *La Boheme*.

This improbable chain of events alone would make for a colorful memoir, but it merely sets the stage for Staffanson's third and final act.

Something inexplicable summoned him homeward from the Berkshires. While on summer breaks from Springfield in Montana, where he savored the return to cattle roundups and riding with his wife, Ann, he forged friendships with Native Americans. Staffanson, in ways he hadn't before, saw for the first time, the intense racism directed at indigenous people by his own culture. And he became ashamed.

As he spent more time in the company of Indians from various tribes, often on reservations, he realized his own life wasn't complete. Far from it. Rising consciousness about the abuses of native people and the suffering they had endured as a result of European conquest left him rattled and unable to feign ignorance any longer.

He told his wife he wanted to quit his conducting career and move back West. In the wake of that life-altering decision, he was beset by sudden tragedy. Complications of an illness would, over time, rob Staffanson of his hearing, the most valuable sensual asset he had. Paradoxically, he says, it forced him to become a better *listener*.

Again, his life would take another dramatic turn. It was only while attending a gathering of Blood Indians at a remote camp in Canada, that Staffanson heeded a yearning for meaning that had been percolating inside him his entire life. He emerged, vowing to devote himself to being an ally to indigenous peoples. Quickly, he discovered the decision would be met with incredulity and suspicion by distrusting Indians and equal astonishment and animosity from acquaintances in white society who accused him of betraying his race.

Oren Lyons, a renowned leader, activist, and elder in the Onondaga Nation (one of the six tribes of the Iroquois Confederacy) and who today has a close bond with Staffanson, told me, "At first, we didn't know what to make of Bob. An indication of his character is not that he sought to somehow gain or establish himself as a self-righteous do-gooder, but it is what Bob *gave up* that demonstrated his intention was sincere. This is what earned him trust and credibility. What he gave up was everything—his career; his power; his prestige and standing; and having to explain it all to his dear partner, Ann."

In the quest to confront 500 years of genocide committed against the oldest people on the continent, Staffanson and traditional indigenous leaders founded the American Indian Institute and originated an unprecedented concept called the "Traditional Circle of Indian Elders and Youth." It has opened lines of communication

among indigenous cultures globally in ways that never before existed.

As Staffanson explains later in these pages, "The core of the Circle is about 50 leaders from the four directions who hold gatherings called Councils each year in a different part of Indian Country in North America. In each place, they meet with between three and five hundred or more people; so over the years the number associated with the Circle, while not quantifiable, is huge. Their mission is to sustain and build the moral base that has sustained their people over time, and through which the heritage will survive."

Worldwide, native languages are vanishing rapidly, and with them, Lyons and Staffanson say, is a profound understanding and orientation, perfected across thousands of human generations, that offers insight to the secrets of existence—for all beings on sacred earth. Today, at a time of climate change (which was prophesied by native shamans centuries ago), rising unsustainable growth in human population, loss of species, nuclear dangers, and culture clashes born by the destruction of natural systems, heeding native wisdom to avert calamity isn't a mandate; it is a choice.

Oblivious to Staffanson and what he and the Circle had done, my introduction to him came in the form of an old-fashioned letter he penned that arrived in the mail in 2013. He sent it from across the same small town, Bozeman, Montana, that we both share in the northern Rocky Mountains. Immediately, within the first few lines, he apologized for not phoning me directly. Mr. Staffanson was nearly totally deaf, a man now in the early years of his nineties.

He had just read an environmental biography I had written about the American "media mogul" and environmentalist Ted Turner, and he inquired if I might help him tell *his* story.

After the book on Turner appeared in print, I had received numerous solicitations. It was only in my own ignorance and lack of time that I initially shrugged off Staffanson. Based on his persistence, he and I agreed to a meeting. We were able to communicate verbally because Bob had learned to read lips and from his own lips he shared an anecdote.

Earlier in the year, he and a visiting Pueblo Indian friend named Jose Lucero had driven out to watch bison at one of Ted Turner's ranches in Montana. The animals were somewhat skittish, Staffanson said, but as soon as Lucero began to sing a Santa Clara Pueblo buffalo honoring song in his native language, the bison—mothers and calves—drew near and surrounded him. Watching it was emotional for both men.

"If you think it's strange, even unbelievable, that this happened and you have no interest in talking with me further, I understand," Staffanson told me. "But if you are willing to continue, there are other stories like this I can share—lots of them. They didn't start happening until I began working with Indians."

I was curious, intrigued, and suspicious. Not long afterward, Staffanson shared correspondence that he exchanged with the great essayist, poet, farmer, and conservationist Wendell Berry. "Now that I have you on my mind," Berry wrote to Staffanson, "I have a question for you. For quite a while now I have been thinking that our use of the word 'wild' is most often used wrongly. From my observation of the so-called 'wild' creatures, I conclude

that they are all going about lives for which the only accurate term is 'domestic.' That is to say that they are making homes, raising young, carrying on a kind of economic life, and, far more than most people suspect, enjoying themselves. And so I ask you: Do the Indians of your acquaintance think of the native creatures of a country as 'wild?'"

Now you, reader, like me, may not have ever heard previously of Staffanson or the American Indian Institute; but I subsequently learned he has interacted with political, business, and spiritual leaders around the world who have been in positions to make a difference for people who have lived closest to the Earth longest. "Native people from this continent are beloved around the world and it's something most Americans don't realize or bother to wonder why," Staffanson said. "I have seen the interactions in Japan, Russia, European countries, and Africa. There is also a mutual recognition of indigenous peoples."

Staffanson and I began to meet regularly and only then did my appreciation of the profundity of his journey deepen. My conversations with him were analogous to the kind of discussion that writer Mitch Albom had with Morrie Schwartz presented in his brilliant book, *Tuesdays with Morrie: An Old Man, A Young Man, and Life's Great Lesson.*

With *Witness to Spirit: My Life With Cowboys, Mozart & Indians,* the book now in your hands, Bob Staffanson speaks in his own voice. And let me assert that he did not need me to be a translator or ghostwriter. He is an insightful, articulate, and thoughtful author who only needed a little gentle coaxing to put his remarkable story down on paper.

Witness to Spirit is not a mere memoir. It is an important, unforgettable book full of wisdom that, once read,

will leave you changed in the way you think about America. It is a reminder for us all of the spiritual transformation that can only happen when we have the courage and moral conviction to open our minds, ears, and hearts.

PRELUDE

Pondering the Meaning of Time

A friend asked me: "Did you *choose* your life?" My answer: "No, life chose me."

No one could have imagined, much less planned, a life trajectory that includes divergent and incompatible elements to a degree that questions reality.

My first steps began in 1921 on an open range horse ranch along the Yellowstone River in a remote corner of Eastern Montana, the living conditions right out of the 19th century: a small three-room house, no heat or running water, electricity, radio, telephone, or daily paper. Conditions that today would be intolerable to American Millennials. To me it was paradise. I learned to ride and help my dad in his work with well-bred horses in an area now known as the Little Missouri National Grassland. Their unrestricted life made them wild as the deer and antelope that shared their range. I experienced the last of open-range horse ranching, watching and learning skills in handling wild horses that had evolved since horses and cattle replaced bison on the vast western plains. The image

and the freedom of open country were so deeply ingrained that later in life I was a bit foreign in cities. I loved the life, but knew in my heart that it was not my destiny.

A passion for music (I could sing before I could walk) led to the study of music and to becoming a symphony conductor, the most unlikely of circumstances given my origin.

My first major life miracle occurred in the early fifties when I was invited to be one of ten conductors in the first conductor's symposium held with the Philadelphia Orchestra under its conductor, Eugene Ormandy. I was the least experienced and the youngest of the group, and also the first to conduct. The setting should have terrified me: one of the greatest orchestras in the world, a hall filled with critics and auditing conductors, and I, having three years' experience with a community orchestra, was first. The first part of the miracle was that I was not nervous. The second part occurred when I brought the down beat for Barber's *Adagio for Strings*—nothing happened; my life flashed before me. In the split second of deciding what to do the most glorious sound I had ever heard emerged from the Philadelphia strings (I was told the delay resulted from Ormandy's European beat). When I heard that sound, nothing else mattered: only the reality of working with the finest musicians bringing a great American composition to life. The third part of the miracle happened when I received the best press and became a protégé of Eugene Ormandy, catapulting me to conducting one of the premier orchestras on the east coast. My career took off.

At the height of that career a second life miracle happened. A lifelong interest in Native Americans began in my youth. On a summer break from conducting, Blackfoot friends invited me to go with them to a Blood Indian

"medicine camp," a time when the Bloods hold their renewal ceremonies and live together in their own cultural setting without interference from the outside world; a time to be themselves. A new world opened to me: a world of new values, new relationships among people, new relationships to the natural world, an absence of prejudice, age bias, gender bias, and a unified spirit that minimized conflict. It was a shock. I had known the surface of Native American cultures but had never been privileged to see beneath the surface.

I found a society 180 degrees from its image in the non-Indian world. A society built on respect and gratitude. Respect for all life and the right of all life to exist. A society that considers all life integral, not hierarchical. There is a sense of connection that says we are responsible for each other and for other life forms and all are equally important. Framing these values is spirituality the depth and breadth of which I had not encountered.

I saw a worldview evolved over millennia containing elements critical to survival in a changing world. A world trampled underfoot by "manifest destiny" without any understanding or feeling about the magnitude of its destruction. For the first time I saw and felt epic tragedy. That impact changed my life from a comfortable, productive and prestigious career in classical music to the uncertainty and risk of a search for a new way to rectify the 500-year-old calamity brought upon Native Americans by Europeans. I left the camp with a deep sense of euphoria and I left a career in music a year later for a future in the snake pit of racism and institutionalized hate.

A third life miracle more readily fits that term. I had no action in it but was its recipient some years after beginning work with Native Americans. During an evening

walk in my yard, a bird somewhat larger than a robin with no known identity landed on my head. I raised my arm; it did not move. I picked it up; it did not struggle. I put it on my shoulder where it rode until I put it down by my house; it flew into the bushes. This was strange but I attributed it to a deranged bird. The next morning the bird was perched on the back of our couch. There were no windows or doors open; the fireplace was closed. Our lab pup was standing watching it, rigid, unmoving. My wife saw it first and called me. I approached it, slowly picking it up and holding it in my hand. It turned its head up to me, its eyes red and with energy coming from them that was tangible and almost palpable. I held it for some time; its bill worked incessantly with no sound. I talked to it and thanked it for coming, taking it out and putting it down in the exact spot as before. It did not fly away, it simply vanished. I did not know how to think about what had happened. I called some Indian friends who were not surprised but offered no explanation. I am from a society that expects all unex- plained phenomena to be dissected until each fits the parameters of science. I carried this shocking experience in my mind, attempting unsuccessfully to do that. Ulti- mately I accepted it for itself, knowing that an explanation on our terms was impossible. My belief is that the bird was communicating to me by the same means that allowed it to enter the house with no access.

I don't know what the communication meant but I do know that it had a positive effect. There was new impetus in my work and I had new confidence. I have not spoken about this to many people, as there is a built-in aversion to the paranormal. The response of most people would have been, "You need help." I have become accus- tomed to the paranormal through work with Native

Americans but this was the first time it had happened to me. I have held something from another dimension in my hand. I treasure it.

This is the story of how forces within me, and forces beyond me, shaped a life journey unorthodox in the extreme.

FIRST MOVEMENT

Cowboys

"Well, we were cowboys, pretty good ones, and we wouldn't have traded places with anyone in the world."

—John R. Erickson, M Cross Ranch, Roberts County, Texas

No decent cowboy is anybody without a good horse. The first one I called my own came with a name that some may find ironic: "Injun." A pejorative epithet especially in this age of enlightenment, yes; just a name then; I was too young to know any better.

My grandfather traded for him with the Salish/Flathead Indians at the turn of the 20th century. I inherited Injun as soon as I could ride alone, at age four, in 1925. Before I had him, my dad would sometimes lift me up, beginning at age three, to ride behind the cantle of his saddle on his horse, me hanging on to his chaps belt. Occasionally, he would forget I was there and ride a bit recklessly.

Injun was a pure "mustang," descended from horses that escaped from Spanish Conquistadors in the early 1500s, forever changing the cultures of Plains Indians. A solid bay, small, maybe 800 pounds, and with hooves so

hard we never had to shoe him. My folks had no saddle small enough to accommodate me so I learned to ride bareback, which is actually the best way to learn balance and become one with the horse. If I fell off, which I did often in the beginning, Injun waited patiently for me to get aboard. If a stump or some object were handy, I climbed up and jumped onto his back. If not, I grabbed his mane and shimmied up his front leg. We fit each other; I loved him.

Injun and I were inseparable until age took its toll. The legs that had carried me wherever I wanted to go as I learned to ride began to stiffen, the heart that cared enough to wait for me when I fell off and tolerated any action that my inexperience brought on began to weaken.

In his last months, I could no longer ride him, but we cared for him until one day he could not get up after lying down. My grandfather came and mercifully released him from a bodily existence that had served him well, the memory of which is embedded deeply in my heart. Even at age seven, death was not a new experience to me. On the ranch, death was a natural thread in the fabric of life. Injun's death was much harder than most. The man who had brought him into our lives was the one who released him. I mourned Injun's passing like a member of the family, which in a way he was. Looking back I wonder what name his Indian trainers had given him. I would have liked to use it out of respect.

From first consciousness, the ranching culture, with the cowboy its icon and the horse as partner, became an essential characteristic of my nature. It hotwired instincts into me that I will attempt to explain in these pages—through my journey in the world of classical music and my circling back to better appreciate the people who predated my ancestry on a vast continent.

Cowboys—real cowboys of the real west, not the poseurs who call themselves "cowboys" and play guitars—constituted the last in a long line of horsemen threading through history: Genghis Kahn's Tartars, Charlemagne's Knights, Desert Arabians, Indigenous peoples of North America, Gauchos of South America and, finally, the last of the line, Cowboys of Western North America. Each developed a culture in which the horse predominated. Without the horse, none could claim a place in history—or in our imaginations. A person on horseback is a dominating figure; not quite a centaur but in ways more imposing, with capabilities far superior to one on foot.

To typecast cowboys as gun-slinging hoodlums or mere "hired hands on horseback" or to over-romanticize them completely misses the essence of that special breed. Cowboys were the last human group whose work-a-day way of life was built around horses. Modern technology means there will never be another. Something rare and valuable vanished when the cooperative relationship of human and animal accomplishing complicated tasks, requiring both equally, became obsolete; it was a giant step in the process through which human beings increasingly isolate themselves from functional contact with the natural world.

When I learned to ride Injun, proud to be a four-year-old cowboy on a twenty-four-year-old mustang, areas of open range still existed in the West. My family raised horses on some of that country along and beyond the Yellowstone River where badlands merge with undulating prairie. We handled horses in ways that evolved over decades from the 1860s after the Civil War when cattle began supplanting bison on the western plains.

From about age six to ten, I helped my dad bring four-

year-old wild colts from the big fenceless open range to our ranch for training. Standing on corral poles, some ten miles from the ranch, I watched as riders emerged in a cloud of dust bringing in a herd of wild horses at full speed, their heads up, nostrils flaring. It was exciting to watch. In the corral the horses made frantic efforts to escape, testing the strength of corral posts and the skills of riders. Dad selected two four-year-old colts from the fifty or so head. He and another rider cut out the rest, turning them back into the second corral where they were released, again galloping heads up, full speed toward the horizon, leaving the frantic colts behind.

As the colts ran around the corral they were roped by the front feet. When down, a rider put a knee on the lower neck and pulled the head up making it impossible for the colt to get up. My dad put a rope around one rear leg and knotted it around the neck short enough so that the roped leg would be off the ground when he stood. Then a halter with a heavy rope that extended over the neck went on. Since horses get their propulsive power from back legs, when the colt got up he could be controlled. I watched all of this in fascination from the safety of a top corral pole, anticipating the time when I would be big enough, strong enough, and skilled enough to take part.

When both colts were up, my dad led in a big, gentle, jet-black, 1700-pound harnessed work horse called "Diamond," because of the white star on his forehead. With a colt tied to each side of Diamond's harness, my dad, on horseback, led the three horses out of the corral, Diamond dragging the struggling colts. He made a big circle around the corral, making sure everything was properly in place and then gave the saddle horse to me. My job? Take the horses to our ranch, crossing the Yellowstone River on a ferry.

The open range methods of handling horses may seem abusive but we did not have time to use the present day "horse whisperer" methods, though I should note that any injury to horses was rare and seldom serious. Good horsemen were as patient as possible with wild horses. It took considerable skill and courage as well as athletic ability to dodge flying hooves, to avoid exerting undue force, and to show attitudes of cooperation rather than domination.

Today's world might consider giving a six-year-old youngster the responsibility of taking two wild horses alone over a long distance of open country child abuse. In the culture of my upbringing, young children were often given adult responsibilities, both out of necessity and to give them early training in self-reliance. My grandmother told me that when my dad was my age, my grandfather tied him on a "breaking cart" hitched to a horse being "broken" to drive, putting them in a small fenced area to train the horse. He developed skills in working with horses and a love of them at a young age, as did I.

My dad felt comfortable giving me the responsibility of taking the wild colts to our ranch because I was a good rider and because Diamond was my security. The colts jerked and twisted Diamond over the first miles but he never lost his balance and never showed any temperament. A gentle giant. When the colts finally tired they traveled more quietly, allowing me to enjoy the ride through treeless grassland. You might also think a child left alone in open country with no evidence of human activity would be fearful or anxious. I was not.

In that landscape I felt at home. Besides, I did not consider myself alone since I had four horses in my care. The scent of warm bodies and the muffled sound of hooves on grass filled me. I felt the energy of my horse through

the saddle leather and saw it in the alert working of his ears. I was with good friends. The colts were not yet my friends but I was their friend with all the empathy a child could bring to their distress in being taken from their home and their companions.

Horses are herd animals with deep attachment to individuals in their herd and the country in which they were foaled. Diamond had been foaled in that same country. Each spring the homing instinct was so deep within him that he swam the Yellowstone River to be once again where his feet first touched ground and he first knew freedom.

No tedium arose in the hours of slow travel with four horses through "untamed" outback. The silence, broken by the small noises of horses, the call of birds, and the buzz of insects, overpowered any sense of being alone. I was at home. I considered all this open range ours, not in the sense that we owned it but in the same sense that it belonged to the animals. I was with animals that belonged to the land, traveling at a speed that allowed me to see details; small things, like tracks of animals, the sculpture of rock formations, sage grouse, jack rabbits, and herd animals at a distance, none of which would be seen at high speed with eyes fixed straight ahead. Since there was no sign of human presence, I could imagine myself an explorer in virgin country, a feeling I had many times.

As we neared the ferry sidling the Yellowstone River, the colts' anxiety increased. They found the chugging noise of the ferry engine and its confined space terrifying. They struggled as Diamond pulled them onto the platform. Their churning hooves kicked up wooden divots from the plank floor. Once the fording was complete, it was a short distance to our ranch where they were tied to heavy pillars

in a shed forming one side of a large corral. They were given a tub of water and hay, but it took a couple of days before they would eat or drink. With kindness and care they became tractable but had much to learn.

They were initially frightened of women. One day, Dad had four colts at the horse watering trough near our house when my mother emerged from the door, her skirts blowing. The horses scattered like quail into the timber along the Yellowstone. Rounding them up took considerable time and difficulty. Because my dad trained the colts with patience and kindness they learned to trust him but they never grew as gentle as barn- or pasture-raised horses.

During my first decade, growing up on the banks of the Yellowstone, I heard stories recounted by old-timers who clearly remembered hearing firsthand the news of George Armstrong Custer's Seventh Cavalry being wiped out on the banks of the Little Bighorn. They told details of seeing blue-uniformed troopers who trailed the Nez Perce and saw Chief Joseph.

Just 30 years before my birth, at a place called "Wounded Knee," a couple hard days' ride to the badlands southeast of our ranch, the notorious bloodbath put an exclamation point on the "closing" of the western frontier. History defines that massacre as the last "battle" of the United States' "Indian Wars."

Sometimes, you can't appreciate history until you are some distance from it. The West that exists in the earliest recesses of my memory still possesses an ancient spirit. For many modern Americans, racing across Montana in their cars today, that sense of this land cannot exist. The terrain rushing by seems a lonesome, imposing place, virtually without people. What we used to call "the country"— rural landscapes—were the places where most people came

from. They originated closer to nature. Not anymore.

In my fourth grade year at Sidney's only grade school, I met Lester LaRoque, a new boy who looked different from others in the class. I didn't know it at the time but his name "LaRoque" and appearance gave him away as an Assiniboine from northern Montana. I had no idea why the other kids avoided him. I just knew he was different; tall and agile with features that set him apart. I became his friend. We played together at recess, developing a close relationship that lasted until the following summer when we heard that Lester had drowned while swimming in Lone Tree Creek. This was my first encounter with the death of a friend. It affected me deeply. I missed him.

Looking back almost a lifetime later I remember only two or three of the children with whom I shared primary school; my most vivid memories are of Lester. Our friendship had a chemistry of which neither of us was aware. I now believe that our friendship sprang from the same seed that led me in later life to work with his people. It was only after deeper association with Native Americans that I realized his identity. It stayed with me. I couldn't know it then, but much of my life would be spent helping his people.

In the early spring of 1925 the sound of the Yellowstone River ice breaking up came at night, as it often did. We were all asleep but, my parents' ears were tuned to the warning signal of distant cracking and booming sounds. Huge ice blocks, several feet thick, would soon form ice jams, forcing the river over the its banks into the flood plain and up toward our house. That time of year my dad always kept our Model T Ford ready to escape to the security of my grandparents' ranch. We had to move quickly, though, to safely cross a small ravine—a low spot in the

road—before the water rose too high. That year my sister became so frightened of the water slamming against the side of the car and the chugging sounds of the struggling Model T engine, that she reached over and turned the switch off. We were stalled in churning, rising water. The engine could not be started. It had to be physically cranked from the front. Somehow my parents carried us through waist-deep water to safety on the other side of the ravine. In wet clothes and freezing temperatures we walked the half mile or so to a neighbor's ranch where we had hot drinks while our clothes dried. Then, safe in the neighbor's Model T, we were taken to my grandparents' ranch where my mother, sister, and I stayed until the water receded, usually two or three days. My dad always went back to the ranch on horseback to take care of livestock. Sometimes chickens would be swept away but we never lost horses or cattle. Once, a cow and her calf were marooned on top of a straw stack on low ground. My dad kept calling her, "come Boss," and calling her until finally she jumped off the straw stack into the water followed by her calf, both swimming to safety.

"Wildness," even then, had a mystique that was rapidly receding into stories. When encounters happened, they lived large. I have a vivid recollection of a man suddenly appearing from the woods and coming to our home for help—his shirt torn and deep scratches on his upper body from an encounter with…a bobcat. How? Why? The details didn't matter. No different from tales of mountain men and fur trappers, who reportedly survived tangles with bears.

The man who got torn up by a bobcat was a reminder not only of what the West had been, but of a time that was flowing away from us, like a log pulled downstream on

the Yellowstone.

My mother patched up the traveler from the woods and sent him on his way. I also remember her removing a fishhook deeply imbedded in the hand of a man who had been fishing in the Yellowstone. In those days rural women needed many skills.

While I remained unaware of it at the time, an innate racism tainted the rural West. To my knowledge no minorities lived permanently in Sidney, but migrant Mexican families arrived each summer to work the sugar beet fields. They didn't integrate into the community, but did play guitars and mariachi instruments at country dances. I developed an affection for them, sitting on the bandstand watching them perform and often falling asleep on the coats left there. I remember my Grandmother Staffanson becoming upset when an older cousin danced with a Mexican.

In my later youth spent on the other side of the state, one black family and several Japanese families lived in the area. The black man did odd jobs in the community and was accepted, but I doubt that his family ever received an invitation to visit in someone's home. I developed a close relationship with a Japanese boy a bit older than me. What I sometimes heard was "maybe they (members of a different race) can achieve more than I can as adults but at birth I am a little better."

Near the confluence where the Yellowstone joins the Missouri rested the remnants of Fort Union, built by fur trader John Jacob Astor in 1828. It wasn't a fort at all but an American Fur Company trading post. It's now a National Historical Site termed "the Grandest Fort on the

Upper Missouri River." At one time, that Fort served as a key point in the development of upper Missouri trade. Dubbed "A bastion of peaceful coexistence" it served as a major hub for the fur trade of the time.

Not all relations between Indians and early traders could be considered "peaceful coexistence," though. My dad often told of seeing a horse "pensioned" in a pasture near Sidney. The horse had earned retirement by carrying its rider to safety from pursuing Sioux, and became one of Sidney's attractions.

Another story, captured in an oil painting by J. K. Ralston, the area's prominent artist, told of a horse saving its rider after a long run from pursuing Sioux by swimming the Yellowstone. After emerging on the opposite bank, having done its utmost in carrying its rider to safety, it collapsed and died, becoming part of local folklore.

Where I grew up there was little difference between rich and poor. At our ranch we had no running water, no central heat, no electricity, no telephone, no radio, no daily paper. Our kitchen was a remodeled homesteader's cabin with a living room and bedroom built across the back. A barn constructed of packed straw, large corrals, an enclosure for poultry, and a log "bunkhouse" completed the outbuildings. When we needed a bathroom in winter, we used a commode or walked through the snow to an outhouse in wind chills that sometimes fell to 50 below. By contemporary standards, it would be considered beneath acceptable living conditions. But to me it was paradise.

In addition to Injun and a yellow cat called "Old Tom," I shared that paradise with a pet duck who followed me in the yard and would come to me when I called him. Out of my boyish fascination with how he walked, I named him "Waddle." He came to our kitchen door early each

morning and I would swat flies for him on the walls of the house, which he gobbled up as they fell to the ground. At night I kept him in a pen made of wooden slats. One night a weasel squeezed between the slats. When I went to let Waddle out the next day, I found him dead. I mourned Waddle as one my good friends.

One advantage of ranch life for a child is the opportunity to relate to a variety of animal life. For anyone who considers animals more than utilitarian objects, that can translate to attachment to a species; for me, horses were iconic from childhood. It also creates attachment to individual animals from any species having something of a pet status. My duck would come to me when I called it, something I have never seen elsewhere; so its death was like that of a friend. But animal loss from sale or death is part of the economics of ranching. We had a barn-raised heifer that became my pet. In my childish play she would allow me to twist her head by her horns, something totally unique in her species. We sold her and I missed her. A year later I was with my dad looking at some cattle on the ranch to which she was sold; she was included in the group we were watching. As I walked up to her she didn't move; she knew me. I petted her and twisted her head by her horns to the amazement of the rancher. I believe animals have sentience to a degree we can't imagine. I was conditioned early to both friendship with animals and to their loss. That helped me in coping with death in the human family.

Not long ago as I watched my grandson, Cody, place his violin into its case and set off to play at high school orchestra practice, I caught a glimpse of my dad's silhou-

ette—Cody's great grandfather who was a country fiddler—and I think about the life my daughter's son will have, and how my own instincts carried me forward to this inter-generational connection.

I come from pioneer stock. My parents were children of pioneer families who came West in the mid-1800s, some by wagon train and some later in the initial runs of the new transcontinental railroad. They had the courage, opti-mism, and temerity to leave a known, comfortable, and predicable lifestyle for an unknown future in a new land lacking those things, and to which they could take only token accouterments. My maternal grandmother, knowing no English, left Denmark alone at age 18 to come to America, making her way to Montana Territory where she had an aunt living near Deer Lodge. I don't recall how she managed the trip but a family story heard many times said that on her arrival, a frontiersman offered her aunt twenty ponies for my grandmother. The offer was declined.

For most of my family, Utah was the first destination. Later, in 1872, the year that Congress made Yellowstone the first national park in the world, all of them came north by wagon train from Utah to open territory that later became Montana, settling on ranches in the Deer Lodge Valley. Both of my parents were born there.

My mother gave me the most love and direct moral influence. My emotional tie was deepest with her. She had a creative mind with an eagerness to try new things and take chances. She was capable in more diverse ways than anyone I have known. It was she who encouraged my successes in self-taught music, enduring endless hours of practice, and who supported my love of books. She was a voracious reader; both of us hovered around a coal-oil lamp reading during my early years. She sang while

working, most often the hymns she had learned in the church in which her father was a minister.

My dad was a handsome man with thick dark hair. Just under six feet with a medium build, he never put on excessive weight. He dealt honestly and kindly with people, with a generous and gregarious nature. He differed from most ranchers of the early West in that he did not smoke or drink, and I never heard him speak a vulgar word. His language, while colloquial, was never profane. This may have seemed unmanly to some in his generation but he was a man's man, he just didn't have some of the rough edges. As a child I carried my grandfather's tobacco cans in my pocket to play adult, but I never had an urge to smoke. Dad was a fiddle player, and his playing was embedded in my ears before I was born. He filled the dark evenings next to the fire with Scotch/Irish melodies that came first to Appalachia and then across the country.

All of us, after all, are products of "our people." The virtues of mine were hard work, strict honesty, a willingness to help people in need, cooperation more often prevailing over competition, a deep sense of community, acceptance of difficulties and misfortune with stoicism and without complaint, and a sense of optimism about the future. If I could go back in time I would like to have a conversation with them about the West, how they thought of it realistically, figuratively, abstractly. I would not judge them, nor do I judge them now; but it seems to me having that conversation would be important. I have developed a different perspective regarding the settling of the West from my association with traditional Native Americans, but in my youth I did not hear or feel any attitude beyond that of dealing with and "taming" open country.

On eastern Montana ranches, which were not differ-

ent from ranches in any rural setting, every family member played a role to ensure the family's survival. Tasks were born of necessity, not convenience. Having a material means was relative.

Our house wasn't insulated and the foundation let in cold air, so it had to be banked with dirt each fall. Single-paned windows collected thick frost in which my sister and I scratched designs. Wood was cut from cottonwood trees growing along the Yellowstone River, sawed into blocks with a hand crosscut saw and stacked for winter. A coal fire was banked at night in our "living room" stove but would burn out before morning, sometimes allowing ice to freeze in the kitchen water bucket.

My dad started a fire before dawn. We all huddled around the stove while dressing. Brutally cold temperatures marked the winter. I experienced 60 below twice in Montana. The record low for the lower 48 states is 70 below zero, registered in one of Montana's mountain passes.

Cars could not operate on unplowed rural roads in winter so our Model-T Ford stayed up on blocks. We used a horse-drawn sleigh, and in the mud of early spring, a buggy. In bitter winter travel the sleigh bed was filled with straw and fur robes were used to cover passengers, including a buffalo robe, a remnant from the time when buffalo covered the land. I remember my dad, dressed in his warmest clothes, his face covered with just his eyes showing, driving the team. Horses in winter were sharp-shod to avoid slipping on ice. On the coldest days my dad used the sleigh as a school bus; otherwise I rode Injun into Sidney.

Winter days on the ranch were consumed with care of livestock. Hay was hauled by sleigh to feed cattle; horses needed less care since they could paw through the snow

for grass, and would run to keep warm. Watering holes had to be made available each day by chopping through the ice covering Lone Tree Creek. Timber along the Yellowstone River provided some shelter for our stock, just as it had done during hundreds of years for Indian horse herds. From first freeze up through April, our routine was filled with activities of survival and with limited outside contact, leading to a common spring greeting among older rural people, "How did you winter?"

When I rode Injun to school, he stayed in a "livery barn," a stable which kept the teams and saddle horses of ranchers when in town. Bill Canoy, a cowboy friend of my dad's, operated the place. Bill's life working with rough horses had left him a bit banged up. He was the best bronc rider in our area. In those days riders from different ranches would get together to challenge each other, not in facilities like present day rodeos but on someone's ranch. Cars were arranged in a circle to provide an arena for bronc riding. Broncs were not saddled in a chute but handled in the open by a group of riders. It was more community celebration than today's rodeos, and each rider had his contingent of good-natured supporters. Everyone would bring food for a community dinner. There was the deep camaraderie of people living in relative isolation and who didn't get together often; and there was fun with children my age who watched the contests from safe positions, every boy dreaming about a time when he would be riding and roping with all his peers watching.

Bill Canoy always came out on top but it took its toll. His bowed legs were a little gimpy and he had scars of his battles with tough horses. He cared for Injun well. At the end of the school day Injun greeted me, eager to be out after being tied up all day. The ride home was always

faster and more invigorating for both of us than had been the ride into town.

In my teen years to early twenties I was a bronc rider, breaking saddle horses for our ranch. One of my hardest rides wasn't on a green bronc but on a "half broke" horse in the high country. A sudden hail storm came up, pelting us with heavy hail. My horse blamed me for the pounding, trying his best to unload me. It was an interesting situation being pummeled by hail stones while contending with a bucking horse. Fortunately he quit; but the hail kept on.

On another skittish horse, I was leading a pack horse loaded with block salt for cattle, which would be stored in our cow camp. I got careless with the pack horse's lead rope, letting it get under my horse's tail, an area he considered out of bounds. He ducked his head, and spun left, catching me unaware and loosening me the first jump. I rode him, but the only witnesses were the pack horse and some cattle who didn't show a lot of interest in my ride. Bronc riding takes balance and skill and a young body. Good riders like the challenge and test of meeting anything the horse can do. It raises adrenaline and is risky, which adds to the challenge. A broken leg in those days could give you a limp for life. But riding the rankest also brought status in the ranch world. "He could ride anything that wore hair" was the highest compliment. Good bronc riders were the elite.

I helped other ranchers with "problem" and "spoiled" horses. During one memorable outing, I was asked to break a "kid" horse from balking at a certain point in the ranch yard. There was a horse watering trough and pump near the house beyond which the horse would not move. When I arrived, the horse saddled with the child's saddle, was standing by the trough and wouldn't budge.

I didn't think it necessary to change to an adult saddle; this would be easy, just show the horse a little authority. When I got on him my authority backfired: he ducked his head, spun right, and bucked through an area of high grass. My legs were too long for the stirrups so it was like riding him bareback. He had me almost bucked off until I noticed a harrow section at the spot where I would land. When I saw the harrow's spikes, even "Midnight," the greatest bucking horse of the time, couldn't have thrown me. I stayed on him and brought him back, still in the child's saddle. I got him to cross his balking point a sufficient number of times to cure the habit; but I learned that a kid's saddle is not appropriate for handling problem horses.

The last bucking horse I rode was almost a lifetime later when ranch life was only a memory and I, then in my seventies, was way past riding prime. My daughter and I planned to use a friend's horses to ride into the mountains east of Bozeman. I rode a mare with a colt left at the stable. We hadn't gone a mile when the mare in one movement both bucked and turned back which had the effect of not merely bucking me off but launching me like a rocket. I landed on my chest in the mud. I was bruised but not hurt badly; however, my pride was demolished—humiliation. It didn't help that at the time I was telling my daughter about breaking saddle horses for the ranch. She said I was bragging; I said it was merely stating facts for the record. Pride goes before a fall.

We caught the horse and I rode her back to the stable where she was reunited with her colt, the reason for her unexpected behavior. I should have known; another element of my humiliation. Maybe it was poetic justice. In my youth I had ridden tough horses. This time the horse won. It was my last ride.

Our brand was Cross-S on the left hip of horses and the ribs of cattle. I still have the branding irons, small ones for colts, larger ones for horses and cattle.

When my grandfather established his ranch near Sidney in 1906, he joined two other ranchers, one of whom had been a buffalo hunter in the area. They ran their horses together, making a very large herd on open range.

Into the thirties Cross-S horses ran on open range that is now the *Little Missouri National Grassland*. In that remnant of the pristine West where horses grazed on land that had only recently been the domain of bison, I developed a deep connection to a land much the same as it was when explorers Lewis and Clark first saw it not much more than 100 years earlier.

In his journal Lewis noted that they saw "Great numbers of 'Buffalow,' Elk, Deer, Antelope, Beaver, Porcupines and water fowls." He noted that the country was "Beautiful as far as the eye can reach…beautiful in the extreme." I, too, felt the beauty of unspoiled land stretching away to horizons of the four directions. To me it was not empty but full. In our area horses had replaced the bison and elk as the dominant wild animal, but there were antelope, deer, and small animals and birds in profusion, making it a community of life in balance that had prevailed for millennia.

Clichés develop from reality and ultimately become caricatures. Unless one has been young, on a good horse in open country, dealing with semi-wild stock in the company and cooperation of like-minded individuals, there is no basis to evaluate the meaning of that life or the mindset of those who personify it.

In the early 1900s my uncle rode for outfits north of Milk River when that area opened for grazing. He carried its memory and its meaning throughout his life. My grandfather and father ran horses in country that still carried Sioux names. Country that stamped them and made its imprint on me in the most impressionable years of my life. My resentment is visceral against those who trivialize that life through romantic nonsense and third-hand revisionism. But it really doesn't matter. Direct experience cannot be transferred by communication or by art. Only shadows of experience can be transferred. The shadows created by artist Charles Russell have made a deeper impression than other artists in his field for many reasons. But among the diminishing number of people for whom Russell's work is more than shadow, he remains our icon. For me Russell's work, either visual or written, is like going back in time. Like going home.

Most of all, I learned by watching to be a part of that environment, working with it rather than dominating and changing it. I believe those qualities were innate within me but it was this setting and this activity that shaped my first ten years, the most impressionable in life, and which gave me strength to meet life challenges. Horses remain iconic for me; in my nineties, I still miss them.

I will end my life in the mountains of western Montana where I am at home and content. But the plains' grasslands have a primal place in my consciousness. The landscape and the life it embodied are ground zero for me.

In 1918 my parents took a year off from ranching to operate a general store at Lane, Montana, for a friend who would be away. My grandfather took care of the ranch, with my dad returning at critical times. Lane, west of

Sidney, was a town in name only, consisting of a grain elevator and a store; but it served a wide area. Unexpected circumstances created a traumatic and difficult time for them. In March of that year a great influenza pandemic occurred worldwide, one of the deadliest on record, lasting into 1919. It was particularly devastating in rural areas of the West where there weren't enough hospitals or doctors; access to either one needed long travel for many people. Sidney had a hospital and two doctors, and both were quickly overwhelmed. The crisis called for more facilities, so the Lane store was converted into an infirmary for flu victims with my mother the nurse. One of the doctors from Sidney would stop by periodically on his rounds of makeshift infirmaries, but the basic care fell to my mother. Patients were there until an opening occurred in the Sidney hospital or until their conditions improved or became critical. Critical patients were immediately taken to the hospital.

Lay women acting as caregivers had a long precedent. In an earlier period when settlement first reached the West and only the larger centers had doctors, rural women were the caregivers. Often there would be a particularly gifted woman in a given area who would be called upon for severe illnesses; but most rural women had some experience in dealing with common problems. My mother had both observed and participated in caregiving. I was once the recipient of a lay doctor's skill. At age two my mother had taken me from Sidney to my Grandmother Hendrickson's farm in the Deer Lodge valley to introduce me to her side of the family. I developed a deep cough, which did not respond to my grandmother's remedies. Alarmed, she contacted her friend, Mrs. Beck, who was the one to whom everyone turned for problems they could not handle. She

arrived and immediately gave me some medication for my condition. She stayed with me all night, after which I was better and soon completely cured. This was a free service—friend to friend—with continuous care until improvement.

The 1918 flu pandemic was a crisis needing everyone who had care skills. Miraculously, neither my parents nor my two-year-old sister contracted the flu. Worldwide an estimated 30 to 50 million people died, including 675,000 in the United States. There were many stories of that difficult time in my family. One of a more commonplace nature involved my two-year-old sister who lost a prized bracelet; my mother found it in the candy bin.

From the Prairie to the Mountains

I've lived on both sides of Montana—as a young boy on the eastern plains and during adolescent years in the western mountains. In 1931 when we still lived near Sidney, an aunt on my mother's side and her husband who owned two ranches and a commercial greenhouse south of Deer Lodge in the northern Rockies visited us that summer. To my ten-year-old mind this was an exciting family reunion.

I went fishing with my uncle in the Yellowstone, and felt grown-up showing him the trails and special places in our timberland along the river. In keeping with the common practice of not including children in discussions of important family planning, I was not aware the visit was to finalize an agreement between my uncle and dad for him to manage a large ranch south of Deer Lodge some six hundred miles west of Sidney.

Several weeks later my mother explained that we were moving to Deer Lodge. Having vivid memories of a

trip to Deer Lodge in 1927, I welcomed the news. It would be a new world: countryside more green and verdant, snow-capped mountains, "soft" water (fewer minerals), many fences made of jack-leg poles, livestock grazing in high country filled with trout streams and game animals, expanding horizons for a developing mind and body, new schools, new friends, and more extended family relation-ships. My favorite horse, among others, would come with us. I was excited.

The real reason for the move was the lingering 1929 Depression. We were doing well enough, at least from my youthful perspective, because the ranch provided a degree of self-sufficiency; but my dad continued to require occa-sional work apart from the ranch.

Usually that work involved horses, but it also included a few weeks in the late fall run of the Holly Sugar Company beet-processing factory. He ran their granulator.

Our ranch was relatively small; in the beginning my family had depended considerably upon the sale of horses raised on open range. World War I, along with expansion of farming in the Yellowstone Valley, maintained a good horse market; but when new war technology made the U.S. Cavalry obsolete, and tractors began to revolutionize farming, the bottom dropped out of the horse market. We still raised horses for a dwindling market but it was not the same. My dad was a rancher first; the Deer Lodge opportunity would allow him to continue ranching without interruption.

Beyond economics, a deep-seated desire to return to the area of their birth pulled at my parents. My mother longed to be near her extended family. While I absorbed all of this indirectly, when asked by someone why we were moving, my answer was "hard times and Mother"; I think

that summed it up. When we moved west, our herd of Cross S horses still ran in the North Dakota grassland, the colts no longer branded. They were either claimed by other ranchers or continued wild.

The mechanics of moving livestock and household items six hundred miles across Montana involved many difficulties. The railroad constituted the only option. Two "emigrant" cars were ordered, one to hold livestock and one for household furnishings plus a small amount of wheat and oats for poultry and livestock feed. Watermelons from our garden were buried in the wheat to keep them fresh. My dad traveled in the household car to be available for care of the livestock. We took several of our best horses, including my gray gelding, and two milk cows as well as our cat, a big yellow beautifully-marked male "Old Tom," who stayed in the household car by my dad's bunk. He was my age and my buddy. At the new ranch he immediately disappeared upon being released. We thought he had run away. Two days later he came limping back to the house. He had eaten a gopher someone had poisoned. We held him and cared for him but it was too late. I buried him with an overpowering feeling of true loss.

My sister was in high school when the decision was made to move to Deer Lodge and had to go on ahead because school was starting. My mother and I traveled there in our 1927 Chrysler. It had no key; the ignition was turned on and off by a switch. We carried only personal articles. It took us three days and a few tire fixes to drive six hundred miles from Sidney to Deer Lodge; for me it was a real adventure and for my mother it was a test of her skills as well as her courage. In those days it was not considered safe for a woman to be out alone on a long drive.

Roads were narrow and difficult, some graveled, some dirt, some sticky gumbo. When they were wet, travel was slow with deep mud, requiring lower gears and the danger of sliding off or becoming bogged down. On our second day we encountered a very wet stretch of road. Our car slipped sideways and off into the ditch. There was no traffic and no one to help. My mother stayed in the car while I walked to the nearest farm. A very accommodating man pulled us back onto the road with his team of horses. We arrived at the next town late and hungry, with Mother exhausted from trying to keep the car on the road. The sun was out the next morning, raising our spirits.

Our last night was spent in a "tourist cabin" (no motels at that time) at Jefferson Island near Cardwell, east of Butte. In the morning, frost covered the land: our welcome to a new climate zone. We were bundled up. As we crossed a culvert under the road we saw a "tramp" emerge from it with his bundle, having spent a very cold and cramped night.

It took a week for my dad to finally reach Deer Lodge because the railroad cars had to be sidetracked periodically to feed and water the animals, and then wait to hook onto the next freight train that would move them to another stop for feed and exercise. This was also a time when homeless men, "hobos," traveled in open cars on freight trains. My dad told of being bothered by some, but he never had any real trouble.

Deer Lodge was home country for my parents, and it became home country for me. I am an admirer of small towns; Deer Lodge is my favorite, not only because much of my youth was spent in its vicinity, but also because its qualities remain vivid after almost a lifetime. Though I was not born there it will always remain my home town.

It is one of the oldest towns in Montana, having been settled in the 1860s before Montana was even a Territory on the map. In my time it had about 3,500 friendly, accommodating, and unified people, most of whom knew each other. It was essentially crime-free. My aunt never took the keys out of her car. It was safe. Having been one of the political and cultural centers of the early Territory, it had outstanding professional people; some of whom built impressive homes on its tree-lined streets. It is situated in a beautiful area with high mountains on both sides of the valley. The town and the valley got its name from a hot springs in the upper valley that built a cone 40 feet high. Its shape, with steam coming from the top, resembled an Indian lodge with smoke issuing from a fire inside. Because the area attracted many whitetail deer, the Shoshone Indians called it the "lodge of the whitetail deer." That was shortened to "Deer Lodge" for both the valley and the town.

John Grant, a fur trader from Canada, established the first ranch in Montana at Deer Lodge in the late 1850s, stocked with cattle abandoned by travelers on the Oregon Trail. It was ideal stock country with grass in some places up to a horse's knees; cold creeks ran from snow-covered highlands, with timbered areas providing shelter in winter. Lush areas along a river bottom provided good hay land. In the early 1860s Grant sold it to Conrad Kohrs, a Danish immigrant who was a butcher. Together with his half-brother, John Bielenberg, they expanded the ranch beyond its Montana borders to ten million acres of grazing land in two states and two Canadian provinces, much of it open range. They ran 50,000 head of cattle on one of the largest ranches in America. My uncle rode for them on the Deer Lodge unit. Over time the grazing land diminished because

of homesteading, leaving only the Deer Lodge property. Our ranch bordered theirs, and my dad became a close friend of Conrad Kohrs' grandson who was the last of the Kohrs family to manage the ranch. In 1972 it was sold to the National Park Service and is now the "Grant Kohrs Ranch National Monument."

Our Deer Lodge Valley ranch was larger by many times than our place on the Yellowstone. Its house and outbuildings represented transformation to a more modern world. Our new home had electricity, running water, an "ice box" and a radio. The addition of indoor plumbing and an electric refrigerator came later.

Out back stood the largest log barn I had ever seen. I spent hours throwing a ball and catching it off the barn's high roof, especially after school when my body needed to run from being cooped up most of the day. There was a log bunkhouse and a hen house, surrounded by large "chicken wire" pens for both chickens and turkeys. A garage included space for a shop where my dad sharpened mower blades for harvesting hay. There were two small buildings, one of which I converted into my own cabin. I had a bed, table, chairs, bookcase, gun rack, and music stand. I slept there in spring and fall but used it in all seasons except winter because it had no heat. Inside is where I practiced the violin.

The Deer Lodge Valley had been an important route for plateau and mountain Indians to reach buffalo country. Because Indian conflicts were still fresh in the minds of living people (in 1877 my grandfather helped transport wounded soldiers to a hospital in Anaconda from the Big Hole Battlefield in which Colonel Gibbons tried to intercept the Nez Perce in their attempt to take all of their people to Canada for safety), Indians were vilified. I

remember no conversations about Indians in our household, but there were stories about Indians in the family background.

During a wagon-train trip from Iowa to the Salt Lake valley in which my Staffanson great-grandparents participated, there were conflicts with Indians. I remember writers sitting with my grandfather getting information about those and other matters of the early West for books they were writing. Unfortunately, I was too young to hear any of it. My Grandmother Hendrickson told of Flathead Indians traveling through the Deer Lodge valley in the 1870s and of the warning for rural people to seek protection in the town. The Flatheads (Salish) had come through the Deer Lodge Valley for countless years to get to buffalo country. The habit persisted even though there were few buffalo left.

My grandmother's family stayed at home, receiving no harm to them or their property. The Flatheads were peaceful people, but the negative Indian image cast a shadow over their true nature. Some years later the Flatheads camped near my grandfather's ranch in the upper Deer Lodge valley. That's when he traded with them for the mustang "Injun." Twenty years later Injun was mine.

I thought of my Assiniboine friend during my own growing up years in the Deer Lodge Valley; I rode with Blackfoot cowboys, one of whom, Abe Racine, was the best horseman I have encountered and from whom I learned much. He was gentle with horses, getting their cooperation by kindness and persuasion rather than the dominance and physical threats of too many riders of that era. He used a hackamore (a type of halter) rather than bridles with bits, which could damage a horse's mouth. He could handle his horses as smoothly with a hackamore as

others did with bridles. Those qualities were also present in his personal characteristics and behavior, making him an ideal companion.

During the summers in the Deer Lodge Valley, I slept outside. My dad put a bed springs near a row of trees in our yard. I covered it with a large tarp on which I put a sleeping bag with the end of the tarp rolled up at the bottom. When I felt the first sprinkles of rain, I would pull the tarp over my head, listening to the rain drops on canvas which were like a lullaby. I came to like it so much that sleeping inside felt confining.

By then, I no longer rode a horse to school, but caught a school bus that stopped at our gate about a quarter mile from the house. Our driveway to the gravel road, which was the main road through the Deer Lodge Valley in our early years there, was lined with trees with a big one at the corner of our yard. It had branches growing out from the center about six feet off the ground creating an open space that was a perfect place for me to sit. When not out riding, and taking part in ongoing ranch work, my favorite activity was to sit in the tree reading my expanding library of books. It combined two of my favorite realities: the outdoors and the mind/spirit stimulation of good books.

When fall came, I ran a trapline in the marshes that bordered the river front on our land and continued it through ice-up. It is an activity, in hindsight, that I deeply regret because of the suffering of trapped animals. But at the time, trapping was very much in the culture of rural boys and men. My sensibility had not progressed enough to question convention.

My marsh sets were mostly for muskrats and mink

with land sets for weasel and badger. I would get up in the dark of five o'clock in the morning to run my trapline with a flashlight, taking about an hour and a half, and returning in time to do morning chores, have breakfast, and meet the school bus. I wore rubber hip boots that protected me in making water sets. Sometimes I would slip and the boots would fill with cold water. I would sit in the snow, dump the water, and hurry home before my feet and legs were frost bitten. The line would be run again after school, the pelts of animals skinned and fitted on drying boards after which were evening chores.

Schoolwork after supper completed a long day. I stopped trapping abruptly when I caught one of our cats in a weasel set. I brought her home and never set another trap. Now I cannot imagine having put animals through that torture. As a teenager I also hunted elk in the mountains. Now I do not even own a gun.

The number and difficulty of my ranch chores increased as my strength grew. By early teens I was doing a man's work on two ranches: our hay ranch and an uncle's cattle ranch north of Deer Lodge.

We raised half-Morgan horses using a forest service Morgan remount stallion on range mares. The colts were excellent cow horses but none of them were truly gentle; a trait probably inherited from the stallion. They had intelligence and spirit as well as stamina, learning quickly the subtleties of handling cattle, sometimes making the exact move needed without being guided.

At breaks between periods of work on both ranches a friend my age from a neighboring ranch and I would take a pack horse and ride to strings of lakes in the high mountains west of Deer Lodge to fish. We seldom saw another human being. We were at home in the most rugged country

of the Northern Rockies at the edge of timberline with snow-covered peaks. In July, snow banks extended down to some of the lakes. We would use snow banks as a freezer to keep the fish we caught. Sometimes when we came to retrieve them they would be gone, tracks indicating a mink had found a banquet. The fish were native cutthroat trout, hungry enough that two could sometimes be caught on a leader with two hooks. It did not take long to catch enough fish for the day, after which we would explore the area, sometimes seeing mountain goats or moose. It was too high for deer or elk. Deep paw tracks in the mud along the lakes meant mountain lions.

Our horses were not as comfortable in the high terrain as we were. We would hobble them on patches of grass to keep them from taking the back trail home. One of my saddle horses would not eat while hobbled. On one trip, with a friend from town, my horse had not grazed all day. He had to eat, so thinking he would be hungry enough to graze and not leave during the short time we had our evening meal, I took the hobbles off. When I went back to hobble him he was gone; he wanted to go home more than he wanted to eat. We decided to pack up and find him, putting my saddle on top of the pack and me on foot. He had a half shoe on the left front foot so he was easy to track. When we reached the lower elevation it was becoming dark. His track turned in the direction of our ranch. Soon darkness was so deep that we were feeling our way. When we arrived at a fence I knew our location and could follow it to a road. The fence posts were barely visible. At one point we startled a sleeping herd of horses, scattering them. We found the road, the bed of which could be followed in total darkness. A dim road branched off it leading to our ranch. The trick was to find it, like finding a needle

in a haystack. After some time I smelled water, instantly knowing where we were. There was a small lake near the turnoff to our ranch; we proceeded carefully and found it. At the ranch we unpacked, and by that time it was about 2:00 AM. We drove into town where his wife was staying with my wife in our apartment. Our reception was less than anticipated from the two sleepy women; my friend's wife had to wake a baby and take it home. They didn't know the difficulty and skill needed to take us from timberline in the mountains and then to find the road to the ranch in total darkness, and at that point they didn't care. I found my horse the next day.

A colorful bachelor cowman, Tom Ryan, lived some distance from us in the Deer Lodge Valley. He was a big, imposing man who liked practical jokes. If you were riding with him and focused on something, he would drop back and flip the end of his rope in your horse's flank, causing him to react and sometimes buck, catching you unaware. Once when some of Tom's horses mixed with ours, a friend and I drove them back to his ranch. We arrived about noon. Tommy invited us to have dinner with him at his place on a small creek (no one called the noon meal "lunch" in those days; the evening meal was called supper). Walking along the creek he took my friend's hat, hanging it over the water; when he grabbed for it Tom dropped it, my friend rushing to retrieve the hat from the creek. That was the first of the "put on" he planned for us. We were kids, about 12. We sat at his kitchen table watching him prepare the meal, including biscuits. He put on a show, throwing pans and taking dirty rags (which he camouflaged, not using them directly). It was not appetizing. When the biscuits came out of the oven, they looked fine, but my friend said, "I'm not going to eat those biscuits." Feigning

shame and anger, Tom took his pistol, slammed it on the table and said "You eat those biscuits!" We ate them.

Tom was a horseman, never walking when he could ride. He raised a small amount of grain for feed, which meant the land had to be plowed and harrowed. Most people walked behind a horse-drawn three-section harrow, not Tom. He rode a saddle horse, holding the lines to the horses pulling the implement. There were many stories about Tom. He would sometimes put people from town on horses that were not dangerous but skittish, a risky thing. He was friendly and affable, always good company.

My adolescent years were spent in the mountains and high rangelands of western Montana working with cattle. Will James, writer of ranch life in the early 20th century, said, "Cowboys would ten-to-one rather be working with horses rather than cattle," with which I agree; but cattle held the economic card, and we did raise and use horses in that work. They remained indispensable partners for whom we had both affection and respect.

The terms "rancher" and "farmer" are used loosely and often interchangeably. Indeed there is overlap but for purists there are differences both objective and subjective. Farmers are more circumscribed. They have a long and honorable history as people who work the soil and who get both physical and spiritual reward from being good husbandmen. They are more sedentary than ranchers. Their focus is crop related, with livestock supplementary. They have a connection to the natural world that has been rewarding as long as human beings have depended upon agriculture for survival. But they do not have a mystique.

Ranchers in North America have a short history, not much more than 150 years. Their heritage began with herders who developed first in the ancient Middle East, roaming their countries with herds, searching for good pasture. The herds were an outlet for movement and a type of freedom in open country that stirred the blood. That heritage came down through history. The focus in ranching is livestock related, with crops, basically hay, supplementary. There is more excitement and challenge in working with large numbers of animals. Horses became partners in difficult tasks that called for judgment and skill on the part of both horse and rider, creating a relationship that was deeper than that of horsepower in farming. A mystique matured around that lifestyle. Physical skills became important and competitive. Special attitudes and protocols developed around both the nature of the work and the deportment of its members, including dress. A "clan" feeling emerged among those most devoted to the ranching ethos, carrying an attitude of being set apart. Undergirding all of this was a love of open country and the freedom it implies. The larger society capitalized on this mystique through pulp fiction and movies, adding guns to the equation. Cowboys became iconic in the culture of the West and a household word in much of the country.

Some of the male members of my family participated in the heyday of the cowboy culture which lasted from the latter 1800s until about 1910, after which homesteading reduced range land in Montana and the big herds began to dwindle. But cowboy culture continued. I experienced the last of the open range horse culture and continued into both the public and private land era of cattle ranching. My temperament fit that lifestyle. I absorbed it with gusto. My dad had all the rancher instincts; I believe mine were deeper.

During my teens music began to dominate my spirit, and I knew somehow that my years in ranching were limited.

I had a little inadequate violin instruction; enough to become proficient in reading music but nothing that helped my technique, which was self-taught and contained elements I had to unlearn later when I studied violin at the University of Montana.

The violin became my lodestone for a career in music. Among all instruments, it is, for me, the best in its ability to communicate the nuances of music. It has an intimacy others lack. Along with its cousins in the string family, it is the heart of the symphony orchestra and has called out the best in great composers. It became, for me, almost another appendage, seemingly a part of my body expressing the deepest emotions for which words are inadequate. Played well, it has the ability to reach people who have limited musical capacity and experience. My wife and I occasionally collaborated with a local minister in Sunday services at the Montana State Prison in Deer Lodge, she playing piano for hymns and accompanying me. The prisoners filled the hall; more, I suspect, for a chance to sing than to hear a sermon, they sang with great gusto. When they first saw me sitting on the stage with a violin they began to make fun using words like "squeak-squawk," and making gestures of derision. But when I started to play, there was silence and complete attention, the atmosphere becoming one of respect. The voice of the violin calmed them like magic.

During my university years, I acquired a violin made by the great French violin maker, Nicolas Lupot, in 1798—150 years later it was mine; it was a wonderful instrument that became a central part of my life. I played it until the

intensity of conducting symphony orchestras left little time to practice and play for my own pleasure. I loaned it to the concertmaster of the Springfield Massachusetts Symphony of which I was conductor, hearing it played under my left ear for all the years there, never losing contact with it. After leaving music I kept it, playing it often for my grandson until encroaching deafness took away the ability to hear music. It needed to be played, so I sold it to a studio player in Los Angeles. It was like a death in the family.

I played in my small town high school orchestra and in a violin, cello, piano trio in church. I also sang in high school choral groups.

When the high school band leader needed a tenor saxophonist he showed me a beautiful gold Selmer saxophone with a plush case in a catalog. I didn't need encouragement to buy it with money I had made from trapping. The band leader showed me the fingering and I learned to play it on my own. Since it was much easier than the violin I learned it quickly. The violin, however, remained closest to my heart, and I continued practicing and playing; but the saxophone allowed me to move in more circles.

The Deer Lodge dance band in which I played consisted of piano, alto saxophone, tenor saxophone (me), guitar, and drums. This was in the late thirties and early forties when touring big bands made stops in Butte and Missoula, and live radio broadcasts exposed us to the music of the day.

Our dance band did not play what is now called "country music." Rather, we made our own arrangements of big band pieces of Benny Goodman, Glen Miller, Artie Shaw, and others. Apart from Deer Lodge we played in Powell County towns: Avon, Helmville and Ovando.

Helmville had a rather small dance hall behind the community center, which took up both sides of the road for a couple of blocks. The size of the hall gave it both a feeling of intimacy and community since it was always packed. Dancers were all local, consisting mostly of rancher families and ranch hands with a sprinkling of Helmville business people. Occasionally there were a few couples from Deer Lodge but no "crashers" from bigger towns looking for trouble.

Most of the dancers were known to each other and many were close friends. There was a table at one end of the hall and benches around all sides. Articles of clothing and other personal belongings could be left on the table or benches with no fear that they would be taken. Babies in baskets would be placed under the benches with someone appointed to watch them. I know what follows will sound obvious to older readers but I'm including it because, if young readers are like my grandkids, they will think I'm about to describe the dark ages. There was more concern about dress in those days. Ranch hands came "slicked up." They wore jeans but they were clean and mostly new, saved for these occasions. Boots would be shined to mirror condition. Shirts would be "fancy," no ties. Cowboys' faces were bronzed from the sun but the space half-way up the forehead would be white where it had been covered by wide-brim hats, giving their heads a two-tone appearance. Hair would be in place with slick hair dressing. Women did not come in gowns but in their very best clothes. Both the dress and deportment of the people showed respect for each other and the occasion, which was a true celebration without "party" excesses. There was no liquor in the dance hall and no off-color language, no fights, no arguments.

Dances would begin at 9:00PM and end between 2:00AM and 3:00AM in the morning. At midnight there was a break. A prominent ranching family with headquarters almost at the edge of Helmville would give the band lunch. We would be seated at a long table set with places for fifteen or more men for breakfast that day. Our food would be hearty ranch food with beef and always fresh pie for dessert.

Dancing after the break would begin with renewed energy. The sound of cowboys' high-heeled boots, sometimes with a metal piece covering the bottom of the heel, hitting the floor provided an enhancement of the band's beat, giving fast pieces excitement and intensity I have not seen since. In a sense our band would choreograph the dance. It was not just the juxtaposition of fast and slow pieces but an understanding from experience of what appealed most to the dancers and how to use both familiar and new pieces, as well as when to insert those of deep sentiment.

On one occasion a male dancer was so taken with his dance partner that he paid us to repeat the sequence so he could continue with her. Watching the people would give us a clue about ending the dance but we never played beyond three. The ending was always the same: we played the standard, "It's three o'clock in the morning, we've danced the whole night through," followed by the sign-off tune, "Good Night Ladies." By the time we packed up and talked with some of our friends it would be about four. After the drive back to Deer Lodge, I would be at the ranch in time to run in the horses for the day's work, eat breakfast, and begin another work day without sleep. I thrived on it.

In his mind my dad believed I should be something

other than a rancher; but I think he had some trepidation about his son having a career in music.

In 1941, I enrolled in the University of Montana Music School, my first break from rural isolation. Prior to enrolling, I had never heard a symphony orchestra. My undergraduate years were an exciting introduction to a whole new world of music. Good violin instruction brought rapid improvement in my technical skill, which opened new vistas, solidifying the violin as the center and root of my musical world. I also had voice lessons for the first time, creating a new dimension of expression that was critical in my later career as a conductor.

My curriculum required learning many instruments. I learned quickly and enjoyed most, particularly the cello. Strings were always my first love. I played in the first violin section of the university orchestra, at one point becoming its concertmaster, and played trumpet, clarinet, and flute at different times in the concert band. I participated in both large and small singing groups, including a small touring group called the *Jubileers*.

I was cast in the tenor lead of an opera, the success of which brought the only serious, if temporary, crack in my goal of working with symphony orchestras. In commenting on the quality of a particular phrase, an opera lover in the audience familiar with New York's Metropolitan Opera told me there were not many notes like that at the Met.

That got my attention.

Voice training and stage experience were immensely helpful in working with singers and conducting opera later in my career. Through participation in the orchestra and through classes and recordings, I made momentous discoveries: the music of Bach, Haydn, Mozart, Beethoven, Brahms, and many others.

In retrospect, I had advantages at the University of Montana School of Music that would not have been possible in one of the larger and more prestigious schools. The UM music department was in a building phase with fine young professors. The depth of my capacities allowed me to participate in all facets of the program, creating experiences not possible in prestigious institutions where specialists prevail in all departments, limiting students to their own specialty.

Shortly after entering the school of music, I was invited to join a dance band, involving the best university musicians, as first tenor saxophone. The leader asked if I could play clarinet, a requirement for all sax players. I replied affirmatively but had never touched a clarinet! I went to a local second-hand store and bought one. Hastily, I learned the fingering at home as well as an adjusted embouchure needed for the clarinet, and played it successfully at our first rehearsal. I literally learned to play the instrument on the job. In a most unusual circumstance, all four sax players were also violinists, giving the band unique versatility. We used scores of the great bands of the day: Goodman, Shaw, and others. While the dance band was always secondary for me, it provided its own special learning experience involving all the skills needed to perform well without a conductor. We had the blending ability of a good string quartet. We could also be creative, sometimes improvising background music for singers.

During idle moments in a rehearsal one of the sax players might improvise a four-measure phrase around which the other players would provide a harmonic and rhythmic structure. It was both fun and good training. We played for dances every weekend, sometimes at the University, sometimes in places as far away as Kellogg and

Wallace in Idaho. For out-of-town jobs we would hire cabs and have them wait to take us back to Missoula.

The university dance band provided a social outlet and a modest income to pay living expenses. When the leader graduated I took his place, expanding the outreach. We had a contract to play nightly during the summer of 1942 at Mammoth Hot Springs in Yellowstone Park when President Franklin D. Roosevelt's announcement of the attack on Pearl Harbor canceled the deal and deeply affected the lives of all men of my age. Memory of the Pearl Harbor announcement and our entrance into the war is etched forever in my mind.

It happened on a Sunday at noon on December 7, 1941, when all members of Phi Delta Theta fraternity to which I belonged were seated at our dining room table. Following the announcement utter silence filled the room; no one moved, stunned for what seemed like minutes. Each of us knew that we would be the first to be called up and that many of us would not return. About half of the people at that table, close friends, did not come back.

It didn't matter whether you enlisted or were drafted. You were called. After induction, I was released because of an abdominal hernia I had acquired during the heavy lifting of ranch work. I was told that if I had it repaired I could be in the Air Corps, my choice. I went to San Francisco to fulfill my service work and have the hernia operation.

The procedure did not go well and ended badly. The hospital in Berkeley, California, was vastly understaffed because so many medical people were in the war zones. My incision was neglected, causing a blood clot in my left leg which kept me permanently out of the military and plagues me to this day.

I had wanted desperately to serve in uniform but instead, after recovery and war work, I went back to Montana and entered my junior year in the university. It was an especially memorable year because it was the one I married my high school sweetheart, Ann.

Frankie Ann Smith and I had a long courtship interrupted by World War II. It began in high school when I was a senior and she a freshman. She was the pianist in the Deer Lodge, Montana high school orchestra and I a violinist. Violinists tune their instruments to the piano "A" note. Sometimes it took several trips to the piano for me to get the proper A. I thought I had never seen anyone who personified femininity as much and as well. Ann says, "He was handsome with a kind, open manner, which was the first thing I noticed about him." Apart from mutual attraction, music was the element that brought us together and grew as an ever deepening bond throughout our lives. Frank Smith, Ann's father, was the proprietor of a highly successful men's clothing store in Deer Lodge. He was affable with a manner that created lasting friendships with all who knew him. Ann inherited those characteristics, which she has used well in our years in classical music and in working with traditional Native Americans. Having been separated during World War II years, after our reunion we decided we could no longer remain apart; we were married in December, 1945, when I was a third-year student at the University of Montana. Since then we have not only been soul mates but also partners in my career in music and work on behalf of traditional Native Americans. Our love has continued to grow over more than seven decades.

That summer, with just one year left to graduation, I worked on two family ranches, taking an apartment in

Deer Lodge. Before beginning the fall term I was notified by the University School of Music that the position of music instructor in the Thompson Falls, Montana schools, about an hour west of Missoula, was open and that they recommended me. I accepted the position, moving with Ann to an apartment in a school housing complex that was built originally for students. I continued studying violin once a week with my instructor at the university in Missoula. I resigned at the end of the school year to finish my degree, grateful for the teaching experience.

Completing my senior year the next fall, I continued through the summer session to receive a Master's degree. I was appointed the first graduate assistant on the staff of the University School of Music. I taught string classes and music appreciation classes, also assisted conductors of both the Symphony Orchestra and Chorus. I participated in staff meetings, sometimes sitting in judgment of my student colleagues.

My first symphony orchestra conducting experience came dramatically when the University Symphony conductor contracted mumps the day before a scheduled concert.

There was no possibility of his conducting. As concertmaster I was the designated conductor with no time for rehearsal. I stepped on the podium without any experience conducting a public performance. I no longer remember the complete program but I do remember that it included Schubert's Symphony in B minor.

Something serendipitous happened. We not only got through the concert, but we played it well, receiving a good response. That single performance, executed under duress, was the genesis of what would become my career as a conductor. Part of the pressure was owed to conducting

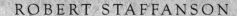
student colleagues—my peers—in whose ranks I had sat for several years but never led.

Would they respond or would it simply be a run-through?

Their rising to the occasion was respectful and synergistic. I had crossed a difficult threshold under formidable conditions, opening vistas for me that had been only dreams.

Falling under the spell of orchestral music in the early years of higher education, I dreamed of one day organizing a symphony orchestra in Montana's largest city, Billings.

SECOND MOVEMENT

Music

"Music discloses to man an unknown realm, a world that has nothing in common with the external sensual world that surrounds him, a world in which he leaves behind him all definite feelings, to surrender himself to inexpressible longing."

—E.T.A. HOFFMAN, ESSAY ON BEETHOVEN

If Ann had been there, she would have held her breath. She would have been nervous for me. Of course she would have seen the audience of classical music critics and conductors behind me and she would have seen the hundred-member Philadelphia Orchestra seated on the stage—waiting for me—when the introduction was made at the Academy of Music in Philadelphia.

She would have heard someone announce: "Mr. Robert Staffanson, here from Billings, Montana, will be our first conductor." This was in 1953. I was one of ten conductors selected to participate in the first-ever American Conductor's Symposium with the Philadelphia Orchestra.

Looking back, I wish Ann could have been there to participate in what proved to be one of the most profound days of my life.

The Philadelphia Orchestra was worldclass, some considering it the finest anywhere at the time. It had been built by the renowned Leopold Stokowski; its fame had been enhanced by the orchestra's appearance in Walt Disney's animation classic, *Fantasia*. The acclaimed string section was burnished by Eugene Ormandy, a violinist, who followed Stokowski as its conductor. Because the gathering of conductors was the first of its kind, Olin Downs, of *The New York Times*, as well as classical music critics from media up and down the East Coast were in attendance. Thirty-five "auditing" conductors also sat on the stage apron.

Maybe there could be a more horrendous situation in which a young conductor from the hinterlands could find himself, but I can't think of one.

That I was the first among ten guest conductors to break the ice for this special event in the conducting world resulted by coincidence.

On our arrival in Philadelphia, the ten visiting conductors had dinner with Eugene Ormandy, our host and adjudicator. I sat directly on his right. At some point in the evening Ormandy explained that he had all of our names in a container. Turning to me he said, "Pick one." I reached in and against all odds brought up my own name. I would be first! In that instant the reality of what I had let myself in for struck me. In my first encounter with a world-class orchestra, a world-famous conductor, and a hall full of critics and auditing conductors on the stage apron, I would be the opening act.

I didn't sleep at all that night. Part of the night was

spent with scores Ormandy had given us and part with worry. This was not what I had expected. Somehow I had anticipated being anonymous in the middle of a group of conductors in a workshop setting with Ormandy stopping the conductors occasionally to make comments and suggestions. Instead we were performing for an audience of critics and conductors. I felt like a fledgling lawyer in front of the Supreme Court.

When I entered the Academy of Music the next morning, I saw the hall filled and the magnificent Philadelphia Orchestra on stage waiting for me—intimidating. Ormandy welcomed the conductors and audience. When my name was called I walked up to the podium without a trace of the anxiety I had felt during the night. I didn't even have the "butterflies" that are inevitable before public performance. There was no hand-clapping as I entered, only silence. We were on display. I was calm and collected, a condition that in retrospect seems surreal. I had the keys to Ormandy's Ferrari. Now it was up to me to prove I could drive it. But when I brought the downbeat for the opening bar of Samuel Barber's Adagio for Strings, nothing happened. My life flashed before me. As if in a nightmare I had no idea what to do. With the baton elevated, I decided to give a release gesture to get it down. But in the split second before I could do anything, the most glorious and most welcome sound I have ever heard emerged from the Philadelphia String section. I was later told that the split-second delay resulted from Ormandy's European beat.

The miracle of the Philadelphia Orchestra strings' sound erased panic and liberated unknown capacities within me.

My life had changed forever.

Early in my conducting career I had felt that my rural

background, lacking cultural amenities and exposure, was a handicap. I did not have the background most conductors possess at the onset of their careers, meaning I had to catch up on a number of levels. Most conductors cut their teeth on classical music. Many had parents who were themselves multi-generation professional musicians, with homes filled with music in which colleagues gathered to play for their own enjoyment. They grew up in concert halls, absorbing the classic repertoire to the point of having much of it in their heads by teenage years. They started early with good instruction on instruments of their choice, often playing professionally after graduating from conservatories and learning from that experience. Most had never left the confines of their urban cultural milieu.

While I had a lot of catching up to do, in the fullness of career accomplishments I realized that my background had a positive side. I was not hermetically sealed in the conducting cocoon or in its urban setting. Ingrained perspectives of a different lifestyle had a positive effect both on interpreting great music, and in dealing with the complicated social and professional structure that surrounds it. I had a fresh look at both the music and the human element.

After completing graduate school at the University of Montana in Missoula, I accepted a position in the Billings, Montana schools on the other side of the state to develop a string program and orchestras in Junior and Senior high schools. That was my foothold for my dream of building a symphony orchestra. I immediately began using the Carl Seashore test to discover promising students. School orchestras resulted.

I mentioned to my colleagues that Billings needed a

symphony orchestra. Discussion with the Superintendent of Music in the schools and with civic leaders regarding development of a symphony was not encouraging, the consensus being that the "cultural climate" was not right for it. The Superintendent told me that an earlier "Midland Symphony" had been tried and had failed. "It would take a tremendous organizer to do that now," he said, making it clear that he did not believe I was the person to do it. I went to Billings in 1950. In 1951 we had the first performance of the Billings Symphony consisting of people who had played in vaudeville and in the aborted first symphony orchestra, plus some newcomers and the best local high school players.

On top of it, I organized a community chorus. The two were combined in our first concert, a performance of Handel's *Messiah*. Its success began a cultural renaissance in Montana's largest city.

Our record from 1950 to 1955 included string programs in all grade schools, symphony orchestras in Junior and Senior High Schools, a Billings Symphony and Symphony Chorus providing a series of concerts each year, and a Symphony Society composed of civic leaders who provided financial and other support for the Symphony, including a manager. That format continues after more than sixty years.

After fulfilling the terms of my contract, I approached School Superintendent Mike Gallagher regarding spending half time in the schools, and the other half developing a Billings Symphony with no reduction in salary. His unprecedented decision to do that may or may not have been entirely legal, but showed great civic responsibility.

However, the decision was not received well by the rest of the music faculty; they were opposed because it set

a precedent they weren't expecting, and established a new protocol; nonetheless, it worked. I had time to recruit new players through trips to the UM Music School and during side visits to Colorado and Utah. I arranged jobs in the schools for new players, and promoted private lessons for them. Two key additions included one of the best oboe players I have known and a fine clarinetist, both of whom had been colleagues at the University of Montana.

Several good players commuted from Wyoming. The Billings Symphony blossomed into a regional orchestra of some stature. Recruiting trips in Colorado and Utah were also productive. One violin recruit from Utah created quite a stir on her arrival. She was a stunningly beautiful girl whose parents were wealthy; she had a wonderful violin, was modestly talented, and eager to start an orchestra career by beginning in Billings. I did not mention her looks to anyone before she arrived in Billings.

After meeting her, a member of our orchestra committee, the wife of a local civil engineer in her 60s, was astonished, and word of this new player spread rapidly. She graced the violin section for a year after which the complications of the new life she had chosen were too much. She returned to Utah.

Our Symphony Series included orchestra and choral/orchestra concerts; opera, both concert and staged; and pop concerts. Renowned artists were scheduled as soloists. Response built rapidly until pairs of concerts on the series were needed to accommodate demand. It was during this growing success in the mid-fifties that I attended the Conductor's Symposium led by Ormandy.

The art of conducting is perhaps the least known of artistic phenomena. Like the music it brings to life, the result can be felt and processed by sensitive listeners, but

its creative dynamics defy all but surface evaluation. Gesture is the conductor's visible expression of the music but its essence—its spirit—is brought out through communication that defies description either by the platitudes of critics or the insights of science. It was Ormandy's opinion that the quality of sound of a professional orchestra is determined at least fifty percent by the conductor. His contention can be demonstrated by the fact that different conductors get different qualities of sound from a given orchestra, but no one knows the dynamic through which that happens. The conductor's impact goes deeper than sound, to the composition's spirit, the way it "speaks" to its audience, involving subtleties of communication that can only be felt, not analyzed.

The conductor begins the process of communication. First of all, one takes for granted his or her musicianship and understanding of the background, style, and historical context of the composition. Beyond that a conductor is the "battery" that begins a circuit of connection which, under the right circumstances, can be overwhelmingly powerful.

A good conductor can make good musicians play well, a great conductor can make good musicians play "over their heads"— that is, with subtlety and expressive power beyond normal capacity. How that occurs is as mysterious as the music itself. The resonance of that alchemy flows through the music to sensitive listeners in the audience, where it is enhanced by their response, creating a feedback to the conductor and musicians in a continuous circuit building from stage to audience and back. Under the right circumstances, that circuit, which defies descriptive language, can create one of the supreme human experiences. It is the eternal mystery of great music brought

to life by great interpreters.

In the years following the shock of hearing the Philadelphia Orchestra string sound from the podium, I have tried to analyze its impact using music's terms. The precision of attack was immaculate, like one bow. Intonation and blend of the five sections was perfection, as was its balance. Its tone had a burnished, resonant, alive sound within the very soft opening notes; the climaxes were powerful and brilliant. But the "magic" of the sound, the spirit that lifts it to a plane beyond our rational minds, cannot be captured and analyzed. In my opinion, this "magic" makes music the greatest of all arts.

If Ormandy was correct, fifty percent of the sound came from my direction, as did the shape of the composition's impact. I felt for the first time the supreme intensity of connection and unity among superb musicians in bringing great music to life, opening creative capacities within me like a floodgate. Barber's *Adagio* weaves a deeply emotional spell, its quiet opening progressing through intensely moving melodic lines and rich harmonies building to a shattering climax. After a moment to allow the climax its cleansing power, the opening measures return, this time with the feeling of an old friend with whom we have shared our deepest feelings; its last achingly beautiful chords are held, gradually diminishing to silence. The baton remains up for moments, allowing silence to climax an unforgettable glimpse into music's stratosphere.

When I left the stage my clothes were soaked, my mind still in the aura of the Philadelphia Orchestra Strings. As I took a seat in the auditorium, Ormandy came back to me with words that put the finishing touch to the most astounding day of my career. With a look of compassion in his eyes reminiscent of father/son relationships, he shook

my hand and said, "I put my faith in you to become a great conductor." It was like receiving an anointment from God. I don't remember my response. He also invited me to come back to work with him and audit his rehearsals, which I did on several occasions.

I don't remember any post-symposium activities or how I returned home. I do remember that receiving "the best press" catapulted me ultimately into one of the premier conducting positions on the East Coast. I didn't return to Billings with an inflated ego, but I did go back with an enormous boost of confidence. I had been validated as a conductor: not with a casual pat on the back, but by the highest and most direct tribute from one of the masters. For the nine-plus minutes needed to play the Barber *Adagio*, I had been in classical music's Valhalla. That glimpse drove me to conquer any obstacles to my return, not just for myself but for the musicians and for the audiences who would share an incomparable experience.

The taste of working with the fine musicians of the Philadelphia Orchestra lingered, and intensified the need to reach beyond the limits of a community orchestra; but it did not diminish my enthusiasm for the emerging program in Billings.

About a year after the Philadelphia Symposium event, I received notice that the position of conductor of the Springfield Massachusetts Symphony Orchestra was open. Springfield, surrounded by some of the best prep schools and private colleges in the world, is the economic and cultural center of Western Massachusetts. It has one of the best regional orchestras in the country.

Wanting practice in applying for a new position and with no real hope of getting it, I sent an application and forgot about it. Since both American and European

conductors would apply, a conductor from Montana surely wouldn't make the first round of cuts. After some time a letter came saying I was included in a group of conductors being considered. That was encouraging, but only as further experience in the selection process. Then a telephone call said I was one of several finalists, giving a date for interviews.

Arriving in Springfield, I was one of seven applicants still in contention; I was the youngest. But I had nothing to lose. The interview process was more pleasant than anticipated, possibly because it was basically a personal assessment with many questions involving my possible interaction in the community; how did I see the conductor's role in promoting the orchestra within and beyond its community? Those were easy questions since I believed deeply that the conductor, the face and personification of classical music in a city, needs to be active in communicating the attractions of classical music to the larger community and within the school systems in order to build audiences both for the present and the future. He or she has a wonderful product to promote: the music of great masters drawn from several centuries as well as the best contemporary music.

We did that in Billings with no successful precedent for a symphony orchestra and against the advice of school music administrators and city officials who said it couldn't be done. In the sophisticated and educationally advantaged society of New England that task would be more pleasant and productive.

Interviews were held in the Springfield Orchestra Association's headquarters in the Museum of Fine Arts, one of several museums located on an attractive quadrangle near the center of the City. Surrounding an attractive

open, grassy area, in addition to the Museum of Fine Arts were a Science Museum, the city Library, a regional museum, and a museum built around the eclectic art collections bequeathed to the city by a leading citizen. This arts complex was one of the finest in New England, an auspicious introduction to the city. Once interviews were over, we were taken to a Springfield Symphony rehearsal of the Beethoven 9th Symphony under a guest conductor. It was particularly meaningful to me, because I had hoped to do the first performance of the Beethoven 9th in Montana with the Billings Symphony. I returned to Montana eager to have the Beethoven masterwork ready for the next season.

Not long afterward, I received a call saying I was one of three finalists for the Springfield post, giving me a date for the final interview; I still assumed the odds were long.

Reaching Springfield on the appointed date, I remember asking, "Where is the hot seat?" on entering the selection committee room. Edward Breck, who was Chairman of the Springfield Orchestra Association and CEO of the Breck Company, leading manufacturer of hair care products, headed the committee. The group also included heads of the museum complex and music specialists in the area. This interview was shorter, exploring issues discussed earlier with more attention to the position's administrative responsibilities. There was also discussion of the conductor's role in securing financial support.

Conducting responsibilities included the Springfield Symphony and Symphony Chorus as well as a Western Massachusetts Young People's Symphony. Each of the three applicants had the endorsement of a major conductor. Mine was Eugene Ormandy. I was told the decision would be made that day. In the meantime I was given a tour of the city.

This was my first introduction to a mid-size Eastern city. Parts of it dated back to colonial times, an interesting combination of very old and new. Residents were most proud of the "old" elements, an inheritance from the time when those elements were a foothold of European "civilization" in an unknown land. New England was a center of real conservatism in a cultural and social sense rather than a political sense. Prevailing attitudes had been conditioned by centuries of tradition in education, culture, and commerce. It had more than its share of great educational, art, and music institutions, and a history of producing outstanding leaders in government; but it was not ostentatious.

In New England, wealthy people did not flaunt their means, but there was widespread emphasis upon family and education background that could lead to class distinction. A familiar limerick says, "Boston, home of the bean and the cod, where Cabots speak only to Lowells, and Lowells speak only to God." Other names could be inserted. I did not find that sentiment to be the case in Springfield.

While cities were not then, and have never been, my natural habitat, Springfield was impressive. Returning to Symphony Orchestra Association offices I was told the conducting position was mine. I stood in shock; there had been about five hundred applicants, many from Europe. I came to realize that Ormandy's testimony satisfied the committee about my musical qualifications since there were no questions about musical skills or relationships with performing groups. Beyond personal interview impressions, I had Ormandy and the Philadelphia Orchestra to thank.

In 1955, at age 34, I left Billings and suddenly found myself overseeing one of the premier orchestras on the

East Coast. When I stepped on the podium for the first rehearsal of the Springfield Symphony, I entered a new world of music. The setting was superb: a beautiful building, part of a Greek Revival Municipal Group at the City's Metro Center, separated from City Hall by a 300-foot Campanile Tower. Symphony Hall had excellent acoustics, a decided advantage for any Symphony Orchestra, as well as impressive architecture. Eugene Ormandy told me that in his experience, Symphony Hall was one of the ten best in the world.

I had thought about an introductory talk to the musicians in the orchestra but as I faced them in the first rehearsal I decided against it. Instead I briefly indicated my pleasure in being associated with them and let conducting be my introduction. The first piece rehearsed was Wagner's Meistersinger Overture, full of Wagnerian lushness and power. For me, its resonance in that hall created an exciting introduction to a new musical experience. My enthusiasm grew with each rehearsal.

The opening concert received accolades as a resounding success. But to maintain that level over time I would require quick repertoire expansion.

I contacted Julius Hereford, professor at Princeton University, who had a consulting studio in New York City. We arranged weekly sessions to study repertoire. I took the train down. Julius was one of the finest musicians and one of the finest human beings I have known. An accomplished pianist and authority on the works of the great composers, particularly baroque composers, he fled Germany ahead of the Nazi takeover, arriving in Manhattan. One of the positive impacts of World War II for the United States was the number of professional people from Germany: musicians, scientists, and others who brought

their skills and learning to our country.

I studied with Julius in his New York studio. We sat at his piano with orchestral scores on the rack. It was not a typical teacher/student relationship, but a perfect John Dewey learning setup: two intellects, together focused on finding meaning in the notes and marks left by great composers on manuscript paper, and determining the best ways to express that meaning. Julius brought the wisdom of long experience and I a fresh and eager mind. Ideas came from both sides; it didn't matter, each stimulating the other. The interaction of two creative minds creates results greater than one alone, and proves much more exciting. My background allowed me to learn quickly, developing a deep bond with Hereford. In years of professional experience, I found that same bond developing to various degrees with colleagues in performing great music, including in the relationships of conductor/players, conductor/soloists, conductor/composers, conductor/conductors and also conductor/audience; but no connection matched the one with Hereford. I was both surprised and gratified to find a greater degree of cohesion, respect, and esteem among top participants in the classical music field than in any other group I have known. Because egos were large, competitive contention sometimes marred the bonds. But if the spirit of the artist matched that of the music there were no barriers; there were only kindred spirits bringing the greatest of all arts to life and creating relationship depths beyond the understanding of others.

While I had a modest background of works performed, every concert of the first years was filled with first performances for me. Hereford marveled at the burden this challenge caused, and how it was overcome. Diligent study and long hours were involved, in addition to which were

the problems of rebuilding an orchestra that had deteriorated and building financial and organizational support from many new people, as the death of the former conductor had given some an opportunity to opt out.

A clean slate is challenging, so new people and new sources of support were forthcoming. Over time we expanded the Orchestra's outreach, extending children's concerts to a much larger area and introducing "Pop" Concerts on the series, conducted by the renowned Boston Pops conductor, Arthur Fiedler. We added opera to the Symphony series and toured the Orchestra in New England and as far south as Atlantic City. Additionally, a small touring orchestra was formed, as well as chamber groups, within the Orchestra. We scheduled pre-concert lectures and developed a local television program called "New Dimensions in Listening." We also broadcast weekly over a Fordham University FM station in New York City. Julius Hereford participated in the "New Dimensions" TV programs, adding his charming German accent to discussion of the music. The program was something of a European version of Leonard Bernstein's educational programs with the New York Philharmonic. Hereford's piano served as the demonstration instrument.

In addition to Springfield duties, I joined the Mt. Holyoke College faculty in South Hadley for a time, developing an orchestra there, and briefly teaching a class at the University of Massachusetts in Amherst. From Springfield I would drive backroads lined with quaint farms and maple sugar enterprises, with occasional roadside stands of fruit and vegetables in season and pumpkins in the fall. It provided an opportunity to breathe rural air and feel a connection again to the earth, but the rural atmosphere of New England differed from that of Montana; it was

more "closed in" by topography and human activity. New England rural areas have the feel of an island or a park in the midst of urban realities never very far away. I reacted well to those rolling woodlands, but I felt restricted without the freedom and release of Montana's open country.

The New England countryside has great charm: apple orchards, tobacco farms, dairies, and small diversified farms set in valleys surrounded by mountains; mountains in name only compared to those of the West. But those mountains create the environmental character. Covered with a wide variety of trees, they provide summer coolness and relief from urban congestion, especially in western Massachusetts, New Hampshire, and Vermont.

In the fall season of changing color, tree leaves provide breathtaking, unmatched bouquets of color covering whole mountainsides, the only phenomenon that chambers of commerce cannot exaggerate. Ann and I would take trips along a northern route called the "Mohawk Trail," mesmerized by the brilliance of color on all sides. In lower elevations swamp maples have pastel colors; in higher elevations the colors would be deep. All varieties of red, brown, yellow, and orange mixed with evergreen trees, a natural phenomenon inspiring awe. In the late fifties and sixties, we saw few people on the roads; today hordes of people make fall-color visits crowded, a boon to local businesses but diminishing to the experience. The color change proceeds slowly from north to south, with October 10 the traditional high point; but even when the colors begin to fade the spectacle remains.

I enjoyed my years in Massachusetts, but I always

felt a bit foreign. Ann became a New Englander, completely at home in all of its aspects. While I have always done well in all the settings of my life's work and have made lasting friendships, I have never fit completely because of the powerful contradictory elements in my makeup.

I fit the professional and intellectual environment of New England with ease, but the rural hold on my psyche prevented complete immersion in the New England ethos where "rural" is quaint, not integral. While that condition was never an open or articulated feeling, discerning people sensed it in ways more subtle than speech. It was also reflected in talks to groups and in individual conversations, leading my friend, Bill Locklin, president of Springfield College, to say of me, "He is devoted to his roots in the West to a degree I have not encountered."

While I was in Springfield, learning that I would be its new conductor, Ann had stayed with my parents on the Deer Lodge ranch. I called, telling her that she would become a New Englander. Excitedly, she gave the news to my parents. My dad, for whom classical music and its associated life were closed books, was standing by. His eyes filled with tears, and he said, "I knew he would get it."

The tears were probably from pride, but also from awareness that family cohesion, family unity in the physical sense was now gone. In his old age, the security and love of the adult child and wife who had been closest to him and who had been at his side in both good and bad times would now be separated by a couple thousand miles with sporadic visits at best. Only now, when I have reached advanced age and have the comfort and security of a daughter and her family who live next door, can I appreciate how he felt.

One of the penalties of age is that younger people have no idea of the psychological burdens advanced age carries. As physical capacities decline, anxiety rises, cushioned by the vigor and support of next-generation family. Even under the best conditions a sense of isolation deepens, but without family support it must become overwhelming. My dad saw this coming but did not experience it long; in the fall of our second year in Springfield, he passed on suddenly from a heart condition, never having to leave his ranch and his horses that were his security; apart from them he would have been lost.

While our temperaments differed, he was in many respects a good role model for me. Scrupulously honest, gregarious and affable as many ranchers were, he lacked one of their prominent characteristics: He differed from them in that he was never profane and didn't smoke or drink. He didn't lecture me, but led through example. That applied also to learning ranch skills; he didn't teach, but expected me to learn through observation. Nor was he complimentary. If I did something well, that was expected. We were not alike; but I admired him, learned much from him, am grateful for and cared deeply for him.

My mother had a more independent character. She sold the ranch when she became a widow, living alone in a small house in Deer Lodge until we returned to Montana. She then lived six months with us and six winter months in the Bay area of California with my sister's family. Prior to that, she had spent periods of time with us in Springfield, fitting in well within an environment, lifestyle, and society new to her. She was proud of my position. In conversation with someone she had said that her son was a conductor. The response: "Really, what railroad?"

She flushed a bit and corrected him. Springfield had

a renewing and stimulating effect; she lived to be almost 106, at which time her heart that had beaten for so many years without stopping, stopped. Her life with its creative capacities, meeting all challenges without compromising a 19th century-conditioned value system provided an inspiration and a moral and psychological foundation for me. I loved her deeply. She was not unhappy in her lot in life, and made the most of it. She sensed the vistas opening for me in New England and her reaction carried only positive response.

As I've noted earlier, my love for classical music developed through the violin, and grew through stages of learning the instrument. The violin became the colossus of music for me from the time I could first hold it in Sidney. It remained my most personal musical expression, my entrée into realms of spirit that held me and edified me like nothing else. Practice was anticipated, not tolerated.

The late great jazz clarinetist Benny Goodman's mother said that in the years he grew up in a New York City tenement, when his spirit was "down" he would take his clarinet to the roof and improvise plaintive music, which both assuaged his distress and let him move beyond it. I empathize with that. The violin could help me through difficult times as well as enhance the best times. I was a "natural"; the violin became an extension of my body and spirit; but because I came late to serious violin study, about age 20, regardless of my gift I would never have the consummate skills of someone who had begun that same training during childhood. The automatic reflexes of complex violin playing need to be learned early. I did become skilled, and could have had a career as violinist in a professional orchestra; but I could not have taken the violin under my arm and gone out into the world to make

a living as a soloist, which had been a dream.

I believe the preeminence of the violin among instruments is not only its versatility and capacity for creating varieties and shades of musical effect, but also because its timbre and expressive qualities are nearest to the human voice. It enhances the human voice better than any other instrument.

Among professional musicians, singers are often the most temperamental, perhaps because their instrument is their own voice: the most personal of instruments, about which there can develop some paranoia. Unlike other instruments, the voice is more subject to the physical conditions of the body: colds, stress, rest, levels of energy, and mental resilience, among others. Its productive years are also finite as opposed to instruments such as the violin. Those years can be prolonged, especially if vocal production is sound, and health is good, but short-lived if not; the result is deep concern for both. Singers bundle up against the weather, avoid contact with anyone appearing to have a cold, and are germ conscious.

They also save the voice. Nicholai Gedda, then the world's leading lyric tenor, who did his first "Rodolfo" in America in our production of Puccini's *La Boheme*, would speak to me only in whispers to save his voice. On the other hand, the late Norman Treigle, one of the great bass/baritones headlining a number of our concerts, smoked constantly and did not take particularly good care of himself; his rich and resonant voice appeared to be immune to abuse, but his career ended prematurely.

Having studied voice and having the experience of doing a tenor lead in a college opera production, I empathized with singers and got along well with them, understanding both the physical and psychological aspects

of their art. Our Symphony series included "concert" opera, a format in which the orchestra is with the actors on stage; the actors interact with each other to the extent permitted by the limited space. The full opera is performed, but with no props and few actions by the actors. This allows cutting the music that relates only to stage action, reducing the total time to concert hall length and emphasizing the music rather than its theatrical setting. In one memorable instance we had engaged Elena Nikolaidi, the famous Greek-American mezzo-soprano, to be our Carmen in a concert production of Bizet's opera. We had only three rehearsals for concert opera: the first with orchestra, the second with orchestra and cast, and the third a dress rehearsal.

Nikolaidi was in the latter part of her career, having done the part of Carmen countless times. She objected to attending the cast rehearsal because it "wasn't necessary"; she "owned" the part and could do it in her sleep. But without the lead singer the cast rehearsal would be impossible, so she reluctantly agreed, arriving on the rehearsal stage in a long gown, furs, and an air of condescendence that said, "I have done this role many times at the Met, it's my signature role and I am too good to rehearse it now when there is a dress rehearsal coming up." She was no help in the rehearsal, generally mouthing her role with little full voice. She didn't make friends. The same thing happened at the dress rehearsal; this time she demanded special refreshments at a rehearsal break. My thought: she is a seasoned professional; in the concert she will emerge as the quintessential Carmen.

The concert opened well enough, her voice was good but she was something less than the quintessential Carmen. Then at a critical spot she jumped pages ahead. I turned

green. I knew the spot to which she had skipped, one which had a prominent clarinet passage. I desperately cued the first clarinet; he understood, coming in on that passage. When he came in, the rest of the orchestra sensed the place and came in accordingly. All of this happened within a split second, with no time to think, just act. In the auditorium and on the tape made for broadcast, what could have been a major breakdown was only a little blip, a half-second of blurred tape that did no real damage to the whole.

In retrospect, that half-second sequence touched the miraculous. The singer skipped pages, the conductor had to know where she landed and what was in the score at that point, cuing the instrument having the prominent musical line, the whole orchestra getting its bearing from that entry and adjusting almost instantaneously. It speaks to the skills of professional musicians and their hair-trigger sense of response to unexpected circumstances. Having had experiences with unexpected difficulties over a twenty-year conducting career, I believe professional orchestra musicians are the least understood and most underrated members of any profession. The event also spoke to the arrogance of some soloists for whom success gives a sense of omnipotence.

Opera was the medium in which I had the most fun as a conductor. The combination of voices, drama, and music included an element of entertainment absent from other forms of orchestral music. Concert opera centered on the great Italian composers Puccini and Verdi, as well as others. Staged opera included the contemporary works of Gian Carlo Menotti and Carlisle Floyd, having simple staging compatible with our facilities.

Sometimes in theater productions, stars align in such a way that all elements mesh perfectly. That happened in

a concert production of Puccini's *La Boheme* with Swedish tenor, Nicolai Gedda. Sara Mae Endich was our Mimi. Other cast members were from New York City Center Opera. Done well, *La Boheme* has great audience appeal, having a compelling story and voluptuous music. Given the small amount of acting space, our cast communicated the spirit of the story with enthusiasm and great singing, creating an enchantment that permeated the auditorium. The superb first-act area, ("Che gelida manina") sung by Gedda, was one of the greatest moments of theater magic I have experienced. There wasn't a sound in the audience, and when he finished, the spontaneous applause shook the auditorium. The whole performance was touched by magic, creating an unforgettable experience. I have heard *La Boheme* many times; but this performance remains special.

Other memorable opera performances included Gounod's *Faust*, the role of Mephistopheles sung by Norman Treigle, perhaps the greatest singing actor of his time. Small and unprepossessing physically, he was a dynamo on stage; his powerful voice was filled with the passion and drama of the demonic character he portrayed. He did not give the impression of playing a part: he *was the part*.

He made the fierceness as well as the slimy deviousness of Mephistopheles come alive. At its passionate height, his voice, the tension of body movement and his facial expression, especially the eyes, made him appear ten feet tall, filling the auditorium with the power of his presence. We became good friends. He participated in a number of our concerts over the years including one in which he sang Mephistopheles arias from three operas. It was an unforgettable tour de force. Unfortunately his

private demons shortened his career, extinguishing one of the great voices of our time.

Perhaps the most joyous evening of opera was a performance of *Die Fledermaus* by Johann Strauss II, which is actually an operetta. A lightweight story is carried by some of the most charming music ever written for the stage. Ours was a concert version with a restricted area for the singers, but they communicated their parts with comic gesture and mugging.

My back was turned, but Ann said everyone in the audience was moving and reacting to the infectious rhythms. I have long felt that the music of the Strauss family of Vienna, which took the world by storm in the late nineteenth century, has been unjustly neglected. I realize it fit a more formal time, but its appeal rested in charm and elegance not seen before or since in popular music. These are both qualities lacking in our time, and while they wouldn't dominate today, their absence as a form of cultural balance is missed. I am reminded of Rhett Butler's line in *Gone With the Wind* as he is leaving his wife, Scarlett, "I am going to Charleston to see if there is anything of grace and charm left in our world." Grace and charm are never out of fashion.

My Springfield Symphony duties included conducting a Western Massachusetts Young People's Symphony (as opposed to the Springfield Old People's Symphony, which was the young people's term for it). Working with young people in music has always been rewarding for me. My affection for them is genuine; their freshness and eagerness are inspiring. The challenges of shaping a musical per-

formance with high school-age musicians are different from that of a professional orchestra, which kept me grounded.

Players in the Western Massachusetts Young People's Symphony came from a wide area rich in cultural resources, many coming from families in which music was a dominant element. They were serious, providing no discipline problems. Friday evenings are a time most young people reserve for having fun with their peers; our rehearsals were on Friday evening. Repertoire was challenging. The first rehearsal of a difficult composition could sound chaotic. At a break a visiting friend said to me, "Where do you start?" (to bring order out of chaos). You start with confidence, tangibly and intangibly expressed, in the abilities and commitments of the young players to master their parts and to arrive at a beautifully balanced performance, and above all with patience.

Witnessing the progress of student players in both mastery of printed parts as well as in understanding of how they fit into the ensemble is one of the rewards of conducting. Most had private teachers to help them with technique, and the orchestra would occasionally be split into sectional rehearsals. The finished product provided both reward and incentive for the hours of practice and rehearsal. Tours to nearby cities were a bonus, providing camaraderie and prestige. But for me the real reward was seeing the music of master composers fill the lives of young people in ways listening to it could not; a seed planted that could grow in enrichment over a lifetime.

To ignite the love of classical music and the discipline of orchestra playing in the lives of young players is one of the great rewards of conducting. Each year some Young People's Symphony members graduated and some new ones

arrived. I was privileged to work with several hundred young musicians during my tenure in Springfield.

Ann was a surrogate mother for the young people. She loved them. She attended many rehearsals and was indispensable on bus tours sorting out arrangements during stops for treats and in keeping everything organized. The Young People's Symphony was like a big family.

Members of conductor Arturo Toscanini's orchestras have said they did their best for him because they didn't want to let "the old man" down. Respect and trust are among the best of incentives. When that happens there is a unity, cohesion, and spirit that radiates, giving performances a spark that sets them apart; that spark was present in the Young People's Symphony.

It's been more than forty years since I conducted the Young People's Symphony. During that time we kept in touch with one of the violinists whose family were our close friends. Recently she wrote to me, including this postscript: "Another Young People's Symphony memory. The chairs we used were folding chairs that had little quarter-inch holes drilled in the back and seats. Some of us violin players used to press our fingers hard against the holes to make a raised bump and then come to you complaining that we had blisters and couldn't play. Any excuse to get to talk to you."

The Western Massachusetts Young People's Symphony was a highlight in my career.

Mount Holyoke College in South Hadley, Massachusetts, near Springfield, founded in 1837, is one of the oldest and most prestigious of Ivy League schools. I joined its faculty to develop an orchestra that could be augmented by members of the Western Massachusetts Young People's Symphony to complete instrumentation not available in

the college. In the sixties it still maintained the discipline and protocol of a more formal time, but cracks were appearing, including in student dress. Some came to rehearsals in clothes seen more often in Saturday relaxation, and were sometimes barefoot. It didn't affect their concentration or performance. I enjoyed them.

Applicants for orchestra membership were auditioned. One applicant was a Navajo girl from New Mexico, a clarinetist. She was reticent but composed. Only modestly qualified, I accepted her and worked with her to help her integrate into an environment totally foreign to her upbringing. She was the only Native American I encountered in New England, creating a bond because of my sentience for Native Americans developed over many years. She always dressed well and carried herself well, but did not share the easy friendship of her colleagues. After some months she was absent, having returned to New Mexico for a break. She came back to Mt. Holyoke but not for long. Her next absence was permanent. Affirmative action had not worked in her case, which should have been predictable. A gifted student, she was isolated in every sense of the word. Abruptly immersed in alien social and environmental circumstances with colleagues most of whom came from a Whites-only background, her loneliness became unbearable. I missed her. She represented a situation that fed my need to do something about a widespread human tragedy prevailing for centuries, of which this was only a small example.

Looking back on a 20-year conducting career, some of its best moments were with young people. Music's muse takes different forms, some of them camouflaged, in those fortunate enough to receive its gift. Paul Rosenthal, a college-age student of Jascha Heifetz, was a member of our

first violin section, and his brother, Don, was our first bassoonist; both were gifted, brilliant musicians. Don, older
than Paul, was the finest bassoonist I have encountered,
with an outgoing, slightly askew personality that endeared
him to his colleagues, enhancing his position. Paul was
more reticent, blending into the first violin section and
giving strength to its back stands. To give Paul an opportunity to showcase his remarkable ability, I scheduled him
to play a Paganini concerto in one of our concerts.
Paganini, an Italian living roughly in the time of Haydn,
Mozart, and Beethoven, was the first great internationally
recognized violin virtuoso. He was also a composer, his
twenty-four caprices still in the repertoire of solo violinists,
his two concertos less played but technically demanding.
Paul chose the second. Rehearsals went remarkably well,
Paul playing with the dash and bravura of his teacher,
Jascha Heifetz. The concerto also went smoothly in concert
until the E string on Paul's violin broke. That happens
rarely, but when it does the violinist gives the instrument
to the concertmaster, taking his to complete the composition and making only a small break in which the orchestra
continues. Paul did not do that; instead he completed the
concerto by using the upper positions on the lower strings,
something he had not practiced and was improvising for
the first time. The notes were altered but they were accurate and the concerto was completed without pause. I am
a violinist; I would have said what Paul did under stress
was almost impossible, and I believe most violinists would
agree. Paul's genius allowed him to make the change
instantly, defying normal limitations. I'm sure all members
of the audience knew something a bit strange happened,
with those musically informed recognizing the register
change; but I doubt that anyone, with the exception of

string players in the orchestra, understood the miraculous nature of that accomplishment.

Genius does not always take positions of prominence but can be hidden in the background among those who hold it within themselves, sometimes emerging under the most unusual conditions. Later, after I left the Springfield Symphony, I heard from Paul Rosenthal who was then living with his brother in Alaska. They built a cabin near College, Alaska, where they lived while teaching at the University of Alaska. The cabin was "primitive" having few conveniences, its lavatory being a small outhouse, the seat of which was kept in the cabin during cold weather to make the outhouse experience tolerable.

In keeping with the brothers' eccentric nature, Paul said he was having a "grade Z music career," teaching and heading a chamber music group performing in Alaska community festivals. Don, he said, was now in California "contemplating his navel." Superb musicians following their own unorthodox paths.

One of the interesting facets of a conducting career in the Boston/New York City axis was association with some of the most renowned people in classical music. I was fortunate to have both luck and timing. Ormandy was the first and most important for me because of his advocacy on my behalf.

During my tenure with the Springfield Symphony, he continued as my mentor. When I sent him a recording of the orchestra, his reply was, "That could be one of the good orchestras of Europe." He was interested in my career, offering advice and encouragement. At one point he said, "You should have a manager, get in touch with Judson and tell him I recommend you." The Arthur Judson Management firm represented leading soloists and conductors of

the day. He had represented Ormandy in his first conducting position with the Minneapolis Symphony, and later
when following Stokowski with the Philadelphia Orchestra. At one time Judson was manager of both the New
York Philharmonic and the Philadelphia Orchestra.
Ormandy suggested referring to him as the "Czar" of musicians. I didn't consider it a good idea to use the term "Czar"
but since it was Ormandy's idea, I thought maybe it would
touch a button. It didn't. I got a reply that said in effect,
"I'm not the Czar of anything and my conductor roster is
full. Thanks anyway, best to Ormandy." Ormandy's plan
for me was the standard one of moving up in the field,
each post being a stepping stone to one more prestigious,
with each action and decision of the conductor being considered first for its career contribution rather than its effect
on the current program. But I have never been standard
in anything. I didn't consider the Springfield Symphony a
stepping stone; I wanted to make it the best orchestra possible and to reach as many people as possible, particularly
young people. I didn't waste time cultivating people who
could be helpful in a career move. When I sent John
Crowder, the dean of the University of Montana School
of Music a particularly good concert review, his reply was,
"You have to decide where you are going to settle down
and be satisfied." I was settled and satisfied. I never had a
grand plan for life; I rode the wave of choices as they came
up. The contours of my life could not have been planned.
When I left the Springfield Symphony to work with traditional Native Americans, I lost contact with Ormandy.

We engaged Arthur Fiedler, conductor of the Boston
Pops Orchestra, to conduct our pops programs; he became
a good friend. We shared an interest in music scores and
books, searching used bookstores together. We hosted him

when he was in Springfield, and introduced him to our favorite restaurants. His query to a waiter, "Who opens the oysters?" was a measure of his epicurean tastes. If the chef opened the oysters, they were fresher.

There were many stories about Fiedler among musicians. One involved a bus accident when the Boston Pops was on tour. Fiedler was in a lead car when one of the busses carrying players and their instruments had an accident. When Fiedler rushed back, his first question was not "Are you okay?" It was, "Can you play?" Fiedler had an active and curious mind and was always great company.

Leonard Bernstein was a supremely gifted man who was aware of his gifts. Conversations often revolved around his dilemma in deciding which of his gifts for composing, conducting, teaching, and writing should have precedence, and which were inhibiting the others. Shortly after appearing on the cover of *Time* he gave a talk in Springfield in which I introduced him. In our discussion following his speech, we talked about the *Time* cover.

He said people had noted that his picture on *Time* resembled Lincoln. "Do you think I look like Lincoln?" He was probably the most outgoing person I have met, and possessed a mind that was never at rest. He was one of the dominant conductors of his time; but in my opinion his podium gymnastics did not stand as a good example for young conductors. Ormandy said a conductor should be a statue from the waist down. I liked that.

I was privileged to meet and know several American composers, most notably Aaron Copland. Copland was self-effacing with a gentle manner, qualities which I found refreshing, particularly among musicians with international standing. We had interesting discussions of orchestra scores. He wrote accessible music, which often included American

folk idioms as well as folk music of other countries. I particularly liked to program his *El Salon Mexico*, evocative of Mexican folk music, an effective piece of lighter texture.

The great musical masterworks, which are the backbone of the symphonic repertoire, need to be balanced by other styles and idioms which give both variety and context. Springfield Symphony programs achieved that in a number of ways, among them consistent programming of contemporary composers. When appropriate, we occasionally used performers from one of the other arts, including a mime whose actions underscored the musical description of the impudent trickster in Richard Strauss' *Till Eulenspiegel's Merry Pranks*, or a narrator in Aaron Copeland's Lincoln Portrait.

A special event was the premiere of a composition by Paul Winter for his small ensemble and orchestra. Paul, a successful jazz saxophonist in the early sixties, developed a sextet, including cello and oboe as well as saxophone, guitar, double bass, and percussion to do new music with a balance of improvisation and the composed. Its outstanding success led him to consider a composition for his ensemble and Symphony Orchestra. In a meeting with him, we talked about how his music might fit the orchestral idiom; the discussions resulted in his planning a composition for his "Consort" and Orchestra, which we would premiere in the 1968-69 fall season, the score for which would be available to me during the summer planning for the fall season.

The score did not arrive. I received it just before the first rehearsal of the program in which it appeared. It was both challenging and interesting for symphony musicians in that it called for sections of improvisation by several first-chair players, probably the first time that had happened in symphonic music. But there were sections I knew wouldn't work. We had three rehearsals for each concert. The first rehearsal exposed the problematic sections. Paul worked on it, providing a new score for the next rehearsal.

By that time the symphony musicians were more comfortable with the improvisational sections and were into the spirit of it; but technical problems still existed. Paul changed it again with a new score for the third rehearsal, which went quite well but still left a few rough spots. The final score was received just before the concert. It was the highlight of the evening; the Paul Winter "Consort" received warm applause as did as the symphony players who had sections of improvisation. This was the first time that music of its nature had been heard in this auditorium and probably in any auditorium. Paul's first venture into symphonic music was a success. The Paul Winter "Consort" continued to be successful around the world with his new form of music, which included sounds from nature and nature's wildlife. He became a devoted ecologist. My friendship with Paul Winter continued, but after the struggle to make the work for consort and orchestra successful, I doubt that he composed another.

My endorsement and support of contemporary orchestral music once got me into trouble. In the late sixties, NBC commissioned a work from Igor Stravinsky, a giant of 20th century music whose early scores reflected traditional forms with new harmonic and rhythmic innovation. He is remembered most for ballet scores, particularly *The Rite of Spring*, composed for a Diaghilev ballet which startled the music world at its 1913 premiere and secured Stravinsky's reputation as an innovative composer. He later turned to "serial" music, a system that incorporates dissonance as an integral part of composition.

In its search for a financial sponsor for the premiere

of Stravinsky's composition, NBC turned to Edward Breck, prominent advertiser and Chairman of the Springfield Orchestra Association. Ed Breck contacted a number of sources regarding the efficacy of sponsorship. I was his music authority. Since there was no score available, any evaluation had to be on the Stravinsky record and reputation. NBC sent compelling representatives to help me make the decision. Reluctantly I reported to Breck that while I could not comment on the quality of the music, being associated with the premier of a Stravinsky composition carried both prestige and showed support and endorsement of classical music. It was a tepid endorsement. Breck became the sponsor. The premiere was hyped by NBC on the air and through the press, including the Breck sponsorship. Breck promoted it locally and regionally. The premiere was not successful, and in the opinion of some, was disastrous. It was the victim of hype and commercialization, one of the negatives of the business world. Had it been premiered in a concert hall to perceptive listeners it would have had a fair hearing and been judged accordingly. But its promotion to a broad public as a major musical event, most of whom knew nothing of classical music and were not prepared for the dissonance of serial music, set up a negative response. It was not well received in our community, and I shared some of the blame.

A distinct advantage of the Springfield Symphony Orchestra was its access to a great player pool in the conservatories of Boston and New York City. Accomplished young players were available; but they were commuters, the larger group coming from Boston. New England winter weather sometimes made travel difficult on the turnpike from Boston to Springfield, occasionally shutting it down. A sudden winter storm closed it on the day of a Springfield

Symphony concert, isolating a complete horn section plus two from the woodwind section and a few strings, causing panic for the conductor and staff.

The program featured two young artists, Peter Serkin, pianist, and Arianna Bronne, violinist in concertos, with the full orchestra opening and closing the program. There was no chance to rehearse new music, we would have to cancel or work some miracle to produce a concert. My concertmaster and a couple other players gathered with me in the green room to decide. Cancelling was impossible because all subscribers could not be reached, and the mechanics of cancelling and rescheduling are horrendous. We would have to go with a miracle. We decided to open with an unrehearsed Mozart overture which could be done with a little doctoring of wind parts. The concertos were a difficult problem. With score and orchestra parts on a table we began frantically to re-orchestrate each score by putting missing parts in other compatible sections. Working against time, we patched an orchestration we thought would work but weren't sure. Finishing barely in time to change into concert dress, we alerted the players who would have new parts and hoped for the best.

All twenty-five hundred auditorium seats were filled with people who expected to hear the music announced in their programs. I'm sure some of them thought it wouldn't happen when they saw the number of people on the stage. Our manager explained to the audience the reasons for a reduced orchestra and the adjustments to the program. It was received well, giving us underdog status. Would it work?

They rooted for us. The unrehearsed Mozart overture went well; the concertos would be the test. Fortunately, soloists are the audience focus in a concerto, the orchestra

being critical but secondary.

An astute listener would have noted the change in orchestral texture from the original score but the parts were present, the soloists excellent, and the audience response exuberant. We ended with a small orchestra piece unrehearsed. Miracle achieved; plus an added dimension of audience respect and appreciation for overcoming difficult odds. The ability of professional orchestra musicians to rise to unexpectedly difficult situations dazzles me. I stand in awe.

While unexpected problems occur more often in Symphony Orchestra concerts than audiences realize, we had one that may be unprecedented. We had engaged Janos Starker, a brilliant cellist, to be our soloist in a performance of Dvorak's cello concerto, perhaps the most played of all cello concerti. Starker had been principal cellist in major orchestras around the world, most recently in the Chicago Symphony, leaving it to embark on a solo career with outstanding success. The dress rehearsal went very well; the cello was brilliant and forceful. We anticipated a distinguished performance. At the first entrance of the cello in the concerto, I noticed much less power and vibrancy in the cello's voice; it lacked the qualities of the rehearsal.

Thinking this was temporary, I assumed it would regain the brilliance of the rehearsal. It did not. We completed the concerto, but it didn't have the virtuosity of the rehearsal. At intermission Starker showed me his right hand, the bow hand; there was no space between his thumb and first finger, as swelling had closed it. On the first down bow he had sprained his thumb, making it impossible to have a bow grip necessary to create normal sound. He had to use minimum thumb pressure to control the bow, playing the concerto in excruciating pain. That he got through it is remarkable, even more remarkable is the cello sound which while not normal for him was adequate to complete the concerto. The adage that says "the show must go on" applied, but at very severe cost. Having never heard of such a bizarre accident occurring anywhere, I'm sure ours was the first.

My wife, Ann, made my life work possible. With her love and support for both me and my work she enabled me to overcome difficult challenges. Her background as a pianist, her sensitivity to classical music, her outgoing personality, and prepossessing appearance allowed her to relate well to musicians and to excel in the social role incumbent upon the wife of a conductor. We were a team.

Ann's given name is Frankie. She was the third girl in her family and was given a derivative name for her father, Frank Smith. It worked well in Montana; I liked it, but on our arrival in Massachusetts it didn't work. The Springfield Orchestra Association had arranged a reception for us. Principals in the reception line were Edward Breck, Chairman of the Association, and his wife, Gertrude, who had not been formally introduced to Frankie. Turning to Frankie she said, "What is your name, dear?" To Ann's response of, "Frankie," Gertrude said, "Oh, that will never do. What is your middle name?" "Ann." "That's perfect!" Given the circumstances, there was no room for objection. To everyone who came through the line she had a new name, and since that day she has been called "Ann." "Frankie" didn't fit New England; I did eventually manage to switch names, but personally, she will always be "Frankie" to me.

During our years in music, Ann hosted both formal

and informal gatherings, always with warmth and a common touch that made everyone comfortable. She attended symphony rehearsals, bringing food on occasion for rehearsal breaks. She became friends with the musicians as well as with many season subscribers. She was equally at home hosting dinners for guest artists following concerts. Cast members always looked forward to dinners that Ann hosted following an opera performance. We had Italian neighbors, the Genaro Sarno family; the grandmother was a superb cook. During the performance the grandmother would prepare an Italian meal as fine as that by the best Italian chefs. Ann would serve it hot after the performance and there were always exclamations about how good it was. On one occasion an Italian cast member looked her in the eye and said, "You didn't make this!" It was too good to have been made by someone with blonde hair and blue eyes. She said "No, I didn't make it but we have the best Italian cook in New England next door." For musicians, famished after a concert, serving good food is always a winner.

Ann not only integrated herself well into the community, but also loved the New England environment, easily becoming a New Englander.

Conductors are in a perpetual state of becoming. And in order to keep evolving, we must continuously challenge ourselves, allowing ourselves to be exposed to others who are at the cutting edge. Ann and I went back to Montana each summer to decompress; the West always renewed me. But to keep the level of virtuosity high in Springfield, I, like my peers, needed to be immersed in what was hap-

pening in the cradle of classical music: Europe. And in those years, the continent was still, even 20 years later, recovering from the ravages of the Second World War.

A summer of study in Europe in 1967 had two destinations: Paris and London. Study in Paris was with Leon Barzin, who had been principal viola in Toscanini's NBC Symphony, and who later became a conductor. Leon, who married a very wealthy woman, had a mansion in Paris and owned what had once been a French King's hunting lodge and property on the Seine River out of Paris. During the week we studied in his studio in Paris; weekends were spent on the Seine River. My hotel was near the famous Arch at the western end of the Champs Elysees. On the first day, I decided to walk to Barzin's home near the Embassies district. Intersections were circular. Looking in store windows as I passed, I realized they were looking familiar, telling me that I had missed the proper exit and was stuck in the same location, losing my sense of direction. Time was getting away, so I stepped on a bus hoping it would take me to my destination. A young black man sitting across from me spoke English and helped me depart at the proper place and I arrived on time. This was a gated community like I had never seen. Wooden walls rose from the edge of the sidewalk probably ten feet high. Doors were cut in the wood with entrances cut next to them that were large enough to allow carriages to enter. Entering the door was like entering another world: the noise and confusion of the city were gone. There were green sculptured lawns and landscaping around beautiful mansions that had been built in an earlier era. It was quiet and peaceful with no one in sight. Walking up to a home that I thought was Barzin's, I rang a bell. No answer. The door was open, so I walked in and said "bonjour," but got no

answer. The lack of security surprised me. I walked next door to inquire; Barzin answered the bell, greeting me warmly and inviting me to his studio on an upper floor. Bordering the staircase was a glassed space, extending the full length of the stairs, in which original manuscripts of great composers were exhibited, including Mozart's "Haffner" Symphony. The Haffner manuscript was clean, nothing scratched out, no rewriting. It was as if it had been done from dictation, which in a sense it was. Mozart's genius was like none other, in that he had the structure and content of the composition in mind before he wrote it. On the other hand, Beethoven's manuscripts had notes and whole sections scribbled out, indicating a struggle in arriving at his desired ends. Both rank at the top of any list of greatest composers; though Mozart was probably the most facile and supremely gifted of all, but he was not an innovator: he just took the musical language of his time and did it better than others. Beethoven took music in a new and dramatic direction, becoming a bridge between the classic and romantic periods.

Studying with Leon Barzin was like being present in a Toscanini rehearsal. Arturo Toscanini was the father of modern conducting and as his principal viola, Barzin, had a ringside seat in learning from him. But "principles" were all that could be learned; the essence of conducting being the spirit and charisma of the conductor, which cannot be captured or taught. How that spirit reaches the players lies beyond gesture and language. Musicality is a given, but translating that from conductor to players differs with each conductor. There is no "system" as there is in learning piano or violin. Our study involved the standard orchestral repertoire, including the approaches of leading conductors, always with Toscanini as a firm base.

I was introduced to the European music world through concerts in Paris and also in Salzburg, Austria, attending the renowned music festival there. At the Mozarteum in Salzburg, there were charming evening courtyard concerts, with musicians in period costumes and candles on the stands. To say that Paris is a lovely city is a cliché. I explored as much of it as time allowed. I asked Barzin about art galleries, and he replied that though he had lived there thirty years, he had not seen them all. The Louvre deserves its reputation. I enjoyed walking along the Seine river and stopping at book stalls, the people exhibiting the European fondness for relaxed camaraderie during breaks from the day's activities. Much time was spent in concert halls.

Leon maintained a fully staffed, self-contained farm with luxurious buildings, a sculptured garden, and a small theater. My suite included a sunken bathtub and walls covered with books, as well as a chain to be pulled to summon an attendant for any needs. Suits and shoes left in the hall would be returned in the morning pressed and shined; this was luxury I could not have imagined. Meals were formal. The service changed with every course. Much of the food was grown on the property. There was an "old world" ambience that spoke to the luxuries and formalities of an earlier time.

Sunday was a day for guests, including musicians who would perform in the theater. One guest list included a Dior designer, a string quartet, and the manager of a Paris ballet company. Conversations with quartet members were enlightening about the status of classical music in Europe, where it was much more flourishing and widely accepted than in America. Because of my addiction to the violin since childhood, I enjoyed discussing violins, violin makers,

and the availability of quality instruments with quartet violinists. In conversation with the Dior designer, I remarked that I was looking for a gift to take to my wife. He said, "You are in luck. We have some things that are being discontinued and are on sale. Stop in at our headquarters when you are in Paris, using my name." I did that; the attendant brought out two garments: a housecoat that looked like it came from a second-rate retailer in America and a blue nightgown so soft and elegant that it had almost no weight. I had to have that gown. When asked about price, both were many times out of my range; Barzin could have bought one, not me.

I held them for a while looking at both; my answer was, "I cannot make up my mind; let me think about it and I will be back." It's been more than fifty years and I still haven't been back.

The most startling conversation was with the ballet manager. We talked about ballet generally and about great dancers. Then came the shocker: he offered me the principal conducting position of his company in Paris. There had been no conversation about my conducting experience or my qualifications for his offer. I can only assume that he had been in discussion with Leon Barzin, and that Barzin had recommended me highly enough that he was invited for the weekend to offer me the position. Every American conductor wants European experience; it is something of a validating process that completes the resumé of accomplished conductors. This was my opportunity. We talked about what the work would entail. The home of the ballet company was in Paris but it toured Europe extensively, which was an attractive prospect. He told me about the company and its repertoire, discussing the dancers, rehearsal routine, and the orchestra. We spent

an exciting hour in conversation about the internal working of a ballet company. I thanked him for his offer and told him I would talk it over with my wife and respond to him.

The change from conducting the Billings, Montana Symphony to the Springfield Symphony had been a huge step up, and a principal conductorship in Europe would complete my conducting resumé. I hardly slept that night thinking about the up and down sides of his offer.

In the end the down side prevailed. If I had been single, I would have accepted immediately; but the prospect of bringing Ann from a comfortable and prestigious situation in which she had many friends to a new country where she did not know the language and in which she would be alone much of the time since the company toured often, was more than I could ask. I had conducted ballet but would have to get used to theater routine as opposed to concert routine, learn the rudiments of several languages quickly, as well as the protocol of European conducting, all of which I would welcome but which would take so much attention that Ann would be neglected. Reluctantly, I declined.

Only a few years later I did accept an offer to form a symphony orchestra in Accra, the capitol of Ghana in West Africa. A musicologist friend working in Africa had recommended me to the cultural officials of Accra, who were intent on developing a symphony orchestra for their country. Accra was a city of more than two million people. The idea of building a symphony orchestra on virgin ground and bringing the music of great composers for the first time to a large population appealed to me. The resources of a country in the process of modernization were enticing. There were long discussions regarding details of

the position with Ghana officials via the best communi-
cating techniques of the day.

In the beginning, musicians would have to be
imported; but they could also be teachers of musically
gifted Ghanian young people, thereby building internal
orchestral resources. In addition to salary we would be
given a house with servants. We were also asked to bring
scores and parts from America. Because this would be a
position where I would not be traveling, and that held
exciting challenges, I accepted their offer. We arranged a
time to visit Accra for final discussion. Because I had
accepted the position tentatively, and as we were about to
get shots for travel to Africa, the cultural committee,
feeling secure in the position, began adding additional
conditions including much more help from America: a
red flag. The insecurities of an African country and the
increasing demands of the cultural committee were too
much. I declined.

We dodged a bullet. Not six months later there was a
military coup ousting Premier Kwame Nkrumah, and
installing a military government which, I'm sure, had no
interest in a symphony orchestra. I don't know if Accra
ever got its symphony orchestra but it likely did not, as
military coups continued to take place in the years ahead.

The second part of my summer of study in Europe
included some weeks in London with Ralph Vaughan
Williams, called England's greatest composer since Handel.
I had conducted several of Vaughan Williams' major works,
and looked forward eagerly to studying with him. He was
very cordial in his acceptance of my request. Upon completing my work with Leon Barzin, I flew from Paris to
London, landing at Heathrow airport. As I got off the
plane I noticed a line of newspaper vending machines all

with a banner headline saying "Ralph Vaughn Williams Dies." Had I not seen it I would have appeared at his studio the next day.

This was to have been the highlight of my summer to which I had looked forward for months. How could I fill my time in London now with no preparation and no plan? I decided to go the Albert Hall, home of the BBC Symphony Orchestra, to talk with anyone there as a first step in finding contacts. The BBC Orchestra was in the midst of its annual music festival called "The Proms," held at the Albert Hall. I met Malcolm Sargent, principal conductor of the BBC, telling him of my disappointment in missing the opportunity to study with Ralph Vaughan Williams. He was both cordial and deeply sympathetic, taking me under his wing. He offered to work with me as time permitted and gave me permission to audit BBC Symphony rehearsals and attend Prom concerts. He rescued me, providing unexpectedly good learning experiences that were different from study with Vaughan Williams but rewarding and exciting.

I enjoyed free access to the workings of the BBC Symphony. While Malcolm Sargent was the principal conductor, the BBC orchestra had several conductors. The most startling discovery for me was how different the orchestra played under each conductor. The best musicians in Britain always played well, but only to the extent that a given conductor could inspire them. When an orchestra has to respond regularly to different conductors, there is no stable relationship and ennui creeps in. Under a given conductor the BBC orchestra could be lethargic; under another good but not brilliant. Malcolm Sargent could make it play like the world-class orchestra it was. All great orchestras thrive best under one conductor, with guests

used only occasionally. The Albert Hall Prom Concerts drew the most enthusiastic audiences I have witnessed. It was the only place where I have seen people bring sleeping bags and camp on the grass to be first in line for tickets for anything, much less a symphony orchestra concert.

The symphony orchestra environment has similarities throughout the world, but also differences both subtle and marked. The climate of symphony orchestras in London was more formal than in America, reflecting their national character. All the musicians I met were cordial and accommodating, but there was an element of formality always present, effectively keeping a certain distance between us.

One was always aware of heritage, custom, and protocol. I found the French orchestras less disciplined than some others and without the "stiff neck" tendency of the British. But Mozart and Beethoven speak with the same eloquence in any country.

I liked the cultural climate of London, including the remarkable opera house built on one of the most devastated areas of World War II bombing. London theatre has a well-deserved reputation of excellence. A very different and memorable theater evening for me was a performance by the great Welch actor, Emlyn Williams, seated on a stool on a bare stage reciting Dylan Thomas poetry. I have deep attachment to poetry, believing the poetic impulse is central to all art. Emlyn Williams' eloquence made the evening mesmerizing.

For someone reared in America's rural west, where, with the exception of Indian villages, the oldest buildings in many places dated back only one hundred years, the antiquity of British and European cities was startling. I stood in awe of 12th century Knights' banners in Westminster Abbey. Serendipity played a great part in making my London experience memorable both in broadening my education and in new experience, but I still regret not matching minds with Ralph Vaughan Williams.

In New England, Ann and I developed deep friendships that continued over the years. Its cultural and social climate was much different from the more informal and inclusive atmosphere of Montana. Our immersion in it was instantaneous, with a cultural shock comparable to the physical shock of immersion in cold water. It sharpened our reactions and led to quick adaptation. Sometimes a western colloquialism would slip out, prompting a response like "You folks use [colloquialism] a lot, don't you,"; it was a polite way of saying that such idioms don't belong in New England. We tried, but were never completely cured. For some the bit of western talk added to the exotic atmosphere my background created. After all, I had been labeled the "cowboy conductor." I remember one board member saying with an air of incredulity: "A cowboy for a conductor!"

Nothing could be less "New England," but it also had a good effect: making me something of an oddity and drawing curiosity about my ability as a conductor. In any case, the label followed me during my career there with more positive than negative effect. The benefit was enhanced when *Look* magazine, in March of 1962 ran an article depicting my life in Montana. It had descriptions and pictures of my participation in the Soap Creek Cattle Company spring roundup riding with the crew and branding calves. It also included pictures of my conducting the Springfield Symphony Orchestra, and a reception in the

"Colony Club," one of the great old New England mansions.

The fly in the ointment of a highly successful opening concert in my first season (Ed Breck, Chairman of the Symphony board, said "It couldn't have been better.") and warm welcome to the city was the ugly emergence of politics. The abject loyalty of a few people, one still involved in the administration office and one or two in the orchestra, to the memory of the former conductor was such that they could not countenance such a warm reception to the interloper who now had his position. To them it was an affront to the memory of the deceased conductor, complicated by the fact that one of them had been in love with him. The leading music critic had written a highly complimentary review. When later meetings with the insurgent group convinced the critic that it was an affront to the former conductor, I never again received that level of support in the press again, in spite of stellar achievements. The insurgent group exploited the friendship that had existed between the former conductor and the critic. My relationship with him over time was cordial but professional. Fortunately the positive reactions of a discerning audience prevailed, but I never had the advantage of a sympathetic press. Down deep, something was tugging at me.

Ann and I spent our summers in Montana on trips to visit family. I also helped friends on ranches, and participated with Montana Fish and Game personnel in projects involving transplanting mountain goats from the Tobacco Root Mountains to the Crazy Mountains, and a bear study south of Glacier Park, among others. In each case I took pictures to illustrate talks about the West to groups in Springfield.

My deep love of ranch life was not shared by all of my ranch friends. Many were content with it but did not

consider it special; some liked parts of it; a few hated it; and some shared my love of it to the extent that they wanted no other life. I believe my affection was deeper because I knew my destiny lay elsewhere. A colleague in the Billings Symphony who had grown up on a ranch said all that he remembered was hard work, a common complaint and a perspective held by many in the larger community: rural life is hard work and holds a total lack of intellectual amenities. I found the ranching environment to be enriching of some of those amenities. It did include hard work; but the work was healthy and not consistently strenuous, which made its appealing qualities richer.

One of the people I most admire is the great writer and poet Wendell Berry. We share a love of rural life that has been lifelong, sustaining us in our professions: he as a writer and educator, mine in classical music. Mr. Berry lives on a farm in Kentucky, which has been in his family for generations. He continues to work it and the farm continues to nourish him both physically and spiritually. When he is away from it he feels displaced. His writing reflects the values he finds in living in harmony with the natural world, respecting the delicately balanced forces that have kept his home ground intact and thriving for generations. He farms it with the least possible negative impact and fewest machines; its organic health is his first priority. He walks its woodlands and along its river for renewal and refreshment. He would not be the same writer, the same advocate of respect and common sense in treating both the natural world and all its life including human beings, without the underpinning of his Kentucky rural roots.

In common with Wendell Berry I have rural roots, but mine are in Montana's open expanses of ranch country. The sweep of natural landscape with endless horizons

nourishes my spirit. I like the feeling of being part of an intact natural ecosystem subject to its diversity of weather, and being aware of the limits of its ecological health. Very early I developed an attitude of cooperation and enhancement rather than control and exploitation, while also developing something of a family connection to both its wildlife and domestic animal life, especially horses. Horses were our partners in a way of life now largely gone; it has diminished under the advent of machines and the transition of ranches from centers of rural life culture to businesses, with all the constrictions of modern commerce and marketing. Like Wendell Berry, I have a feeling of displacement when I'm away from my roots. The urban areas necessary for pursuit of my classical music profession were enjoyed for what they offered, and I fit them well; but I was always a bit foreign. The suffocation of urban life was relieved each year by summer vacations in Montana ranch land.

While growing up, my home towns were small communities that had my loyalty and affection; I always assumed everyone from those communities shared my feelings. During my conducting tenure in Springfield, a musical theater production having a singer who was born in my home town of Sidney, Montana, appeared in one of our theaters. After the show I went backstage excitedly to meet a compatriot from Sidney, expressing my pleasure in the unlikely circumstance of finding two professional musicians with Sidney background. My reception was tepid. Undaunted, I went on to say that I would be visiting Sidney that summer. Her reply was, "Really, *why?*" Like a slap in the face, her words ended our conversation and any illusion that my affection for small towns was widely shared. Instead of new friends, we left as strangers. In her

defense, she was preoccupied with going to dinner with Howard Keel, and was not happy to be reminded of a background she wanted to forget.

A profound sense of "place" is, I believe, uncommon. My late sister, who grew up with me in the same environment and under the same conditions, welcomed leaving Montana. She returned only infrequently for family affairs, believing her urban setting in the San Francisco peninsula was the perfect environment. She had no ties even of sentiment to Montana. On the occasion of an appearance of the Philadelphia Orchestra in Springfield, Massachusetts, I took Eugene Ormandy for a ride in the western Massachusetts countryside. He was tentatively looking for a vacation home site, and would often remark, "That would be a good place for a house." The immediate surroundings were important, but they could be in any setting. There was no sense of "place," of the importance of a given area for its own sake or for its meaning in terms of one's values. An individual's occupational and social values most often determine the satisfaction of their setting. Less frequently the environment itself conditions those values.

A lifelong frustration has been my inability to communicate the overpowering subjective influences on my life and their sometimes spectacular results except through inadequate words. Language is a marvelous gift, but is almost totally inadequate in communicating experience in anything deeper than surface. It is impossible to communicate the depth of insight from great music, especially from conducting great music, and it is equally impossible to communicate the realities of a new world for me after a

week in the 1960s with the Blood Indians of Canada as the only non-Indian in their "medicine" camp. In years of promoting support for not-for-profit enterprises benefiting both classical music and understanding of traditional Native Americans, I have done a great deal of writing; all of it plausible and rational, but none of it reaches essences that are the transforming agents. Perhaps that is as it should be. If depth of experience could be communicated in words, the effort needed to reach elevated states of being would be removed, reducing both their impact and the satisfaction of achievement; but I continue to try because of a fullness that needs to be shared.

A number of people who understand the complexities of conducting have said to me, "I don't understand how anyone would want to be a conductor." Conducting is often overwhelmed by overriding elements. Conductors of professional orchestras have a hundred temperamental people to work with and to integrate into a cohesive unit that brings out the best in each. Among them are one or two who think they should be in your spot; an audience, in our case twenty-five hundred people, all of whom have definite ideas of what music they like and do not like; a board of trustees who may or may not have musical sensitivity but who man the financial gates; critics who have biases and may or may not like you (there is the adage that says critics are like fleas on a dog, they live off the dog but don't do much for its health); and tenure that is dependent upon serving a variety of often conflicting interests, something like herding cats.

If one has the temperament and skill to manage

peripheral challenges, the reward of conducting is bringing to life great works of universal composers whose music spans centuries, along with that of promising new composers, with emphasis on the former. Because their contributions are active, the conductor and players benefit more from great music than do passive listeners; but for both players and audience, music in its highest form opens spiritual windows like no other art. For me, conducting is the highest privilege in the arts. I am a better and more complete person for years spent in conducting.

When one is involved with more than 200 instrumentalists and singers of differing races, ethnicities, genders, and ages, working together to bring life to a Brahms Requiem, Verdi Requiem, or Beethoven Ninth Symphony, among others, there is a spirit that engulfs all people with a blanket of love that is beyond our normal capacities. There is connection transcending all differences set up by society; a unity that testifies to the "oneness" of human beings and belies the divisions of hate and domination so prevalent in our world. Looking into the faces of a hundred singers, along with instrumentalists, all focused on communicating the spirit of great music, and feeling the energy of response from an audience, is testimony to the grandeur and nobility of human beings. Its release of spiritual energy and insight is overwhelming. The presence of voices adds a special dimension, but all great music carries that potential. With repetition throughout the orchestral library it becomes endemic to spirit and soul. I am convinced that I could not have worked as effectively with traditional Native Americans without that background.

In his great book, *The Real Toscanini* (Amadeus, 2012), Cesare Civetta quotes several prominent artists regarding

the impact of music in their lives. Lotte Lehman, eminent dramatic soprano of the early 20th century said this about the experience of singing under conductor Arturo Toscanini: "I shall never forget the feeling of intoxication and utter abandon as I sang the last words of Isolde (Wagner's *Tristan and Isolde*). The music was like an overpowering surf, in which I sang, lost in the splendor of sound. And so I feel the overpowering strength of his magical personality is akin to the power of the ocean." William Warfield, bass/baritone of my generation said: "Many times when I am singing, I feel that I am a vessel which this talent is going through. The only thing I can brag about is that I didn't sit and go to waste; that I did something about it and learned how I could be a vessel which God flows through." Leontyne Pryce, great Lyrico spinto soprano, who was married to William Warfield, said: "We are closest to God when we are practicing our profession." Marian Anderson, outstanding African/American contralto who broke barriers for members of her race in the first half of the 20th century, said: "When I'm out there singing, God is with me and is helping me, and that's why I don't say, 'I sang a concert'; I say, 'we sang a concert.'"

The testimony of these artists, and many others, reflects the ability of great music to lift our spirits to heights beyond human limitations to a point that the only reference is connection with God, or in Lotte Lehman's case, the overpowering natural force of the ocean. William Warfield said: "My art and my religion, they're all the same." I have known many musicians for whom music is their religion. I share with all of these artists their overwhelming experience of music as a spiritual force; for me it is not a religion, but rather an extension of my religion, making it compelling in ways that dogma cannot.

I believe great music is a primal force. It takes us beyond the confines of our world into realms of pure spirit: a harbinger of what may be ahead for us.

The summers Ann and I spent in Montana kept me grounded. And, during one of those journeys back home for grounding and renewal, something completely unexpected happened.

As I have described, early in my life I had had experiences with Indians, particularly riding with Blackfoot cowboys as a teenager and later visiting with friends on a number of reservations during summer breaks from the symphony concert season. I particularly enjoyed visiting the Piegan Blackfoot reservation in its magnificent setting: snowcapped Glacier Park mountains in the west; a continuation of the Rocky Mountain front to the north and south; to the east was high rolling and verdant prairie country, much of it unchanged and pristine. I related well to it and to the people who called it home. Indian friends guided me in exploring much of the area. Having grown up with horses and with a love of open country, I felt at home with both the people and their environment; but there was something deeper and only dimly perceived that drew me not only to the Blackfoot people but also other Indians of Montana: Crows, Northern Cheyenne, Chippewa-Cree, Assiniboine, Gros Ventre, Salish/Flathead. It had the feel of family connection. Reflection tells me it was the beginning of a spiritual connection deeper than race, culture, or any of the barriers that separate people of diverse origin.

An interest in Native American art and artifacts made me a frequent visitor to the Museum of the Plains Indians

in Browning. One of its curators was Nora Spanish, an attractive middle-aged woman steeped in the culture and lifeways of her Blackfoot people. We became good friends. Through her I met her husband, Willie Spanish, with whom I had long discussions. He sensed in me an attitude of respect and genuine empathy, and spoke candidly with me about his life and that of his people. A trust relationship developed through our visits each summer.

As I developed close relationships with Montana Indians, an inner compulsion that began in my friendship with Lester LaRoque, an Assiniboine Indian in my fourth-grade class, drew me ever deeper into the world of traditional Native Americans. It is a world governed by spirit more than by material well-being. It does not consider the natural world as something set apart, but rather as a connection in a web that includes all forms of life, all of which deserve sanctity. That perspective resonated with my worldview, which had begun in a setting in which the natural world predominated. The external elements of my life differed from those of Native Americans; but the inner elements, those that give meaning to life, had much in common. I was drawn to their inclusiveness within the human family and their relationship to the natural world, which had a level of understanding and sophistication that was absent in my world. The spiritual windows opened by great classical music fit that inclusive mindset, creating a perspective on the relationship of all life with cooperation and integration replacing greed and avarice.

The motive to move on to a new realm of spirit had been growing within me over the years and was climaxed by a time with the Blood Indians in Canada in the late 1960s. But ties within the field of classical music, close friends in our community, and the prospect of leaving the world of

Mozart and Beethoven made it less than a slam dunk.

My growing understanding of the spiritual qualities of Native American worldviews also carried an awareness of the larger society's ignorance of this defining characteristic and the destructive results of its efforts to stamp out any vestige of Indian cultures. Following the Civil War there was focus on the children: "Kill the Indian and save the child," was the motto. Blinded by the seduction of science and a new world of comfort and ease, they had no clue about the ancient wisdom they were mindlessly destroying. But in spite of an all-out effort to destroy the only wisdom indigenous to this hemisphere, it went underground and was kept intact by scattered segments of traditional society. It was to these survivors that my mind and spirit turned.

The idea of abandoning the world of classical music, including friendships made richer because of shared experience in its transforming power, created the deepest enigma of my life. I had reached a level of accomplishment in a difficult field that could have carried me to greater heights. That I would even consider leaving it for an unknown future was inconceivable to my colleagues. What they didn't know was the spiritual dimension in my decision. I was never hermetically sealed in the conducting cocoon, so I was open to other spiritual influences, which I found in traditional Native Americans. I was drawn both to the inclusive dimension of their spirituality and to the tragedy of their relegation to society's lowest echelon.

Following my return from a time with the Blood Indians in Canada, Ann knew our days in music were numbered. We talked about it first in abstract terms, then more directly. While she did not encourage a dramatic life change, she did not resist it. Few, if any, women would have willingly left our life in Springfield for a new one chasing only an idea with an uncertain future, no prestige, and no security. That she did so was testimony to her commitment and her understanding of the intense inner force that led me to abandon a profession in which I was successful for an idea of addressing America's oldest moral problem: its indefensible treatment of Native Americans.

The surface of Native American life had been before the public since the beginning of mass media. Artists George Catlin and Karl Bodmer were among the first to paint them. Dime novels, and later movies, either romanticized them as "Noble Redmen" or "Murderous Villains" who resisted the intrusion of White settlers and miners to whom "manifest destiny" had given a right to Indian land. The result was a schizophrenic attitude toward Native Americans containing varying elements of guilt, hate, fear, pity, contempt, and grudging admiration for the color and "quaintness" of ancient cultures.

Absent was any real evaluation and respect for Indians as human beings, and total ignorance of the deep spiritual underpinnings of their cultures. When I accepted the invitation to the Blood camp my attitude was one of respect and admiration, but I was as ignorant of the spiritual dimensions of their cultures as my colleagues. That changed.

I left all the advantages of a successful profession and commitment to a great art that had filled me from childhood, to then meet the greatest challenge of my life: finding a new way to mitigate the tragedy of America's destruction of its original inhabitants, and in that process to help create parity among the races and respect and honor for the keepers of the indigenous heritage.

THIRD MOVEMENT

Indians

"The refusal to acknowledge this history of oppression, violence, and genocide, may be the most disturbing and terrible tendency of America's dominant culture."
—NOAM CHOMSKY

"We don't see any spirituality in your world." "We don't see any spirituality in your government, your commerce, your education, your religion; anywhere." "We think we can help you."

These words were spoken to me in a tipi encampment of thirty-five traditional Native Americans from the four directions of North America. Stark and startling statements made during a meeting I had called. In my mind, we were there to explore how the relationship between Native Americans and the people who replaced them might be rectified, and how we might plan a course of action on their terms to accomplish that. Their words identified what to them was a root cause of the conflict: incompatible worldviews, theirs having a spiritual base, ours a material base. They also said the most devastating things that hap-

pened to them were dispossession and genocide, the church, and alcohol. I was prepared for two of them but the church surprised me. They explained that representatives of the church were their first contacts with invading Europeans, gaining their friendship and confidence; but the church was the opening wedge that allowed all the negatives of dispossession, broken treaties and alcohol to enter.

Our encampment was at the confluence of three rivers, the Gallatin, Madison, and Jefferson, which join to form the Missouri river in Montana. A spot where Meriwether Lewis, William Clark, and their Shoshone guide, Sacajawea, had passed through 170-odd years earlier. Sacajawea was born in the area of the headwaters. It had been a common hunting ground for a number of tribes. The mine nearby was carbon-dated to some 1,200 years earlier.

The land where we were camped was owned by a lady who had graciously given permission for our use. Several joined me in meeting our host and thanking her for her kindness. We talked of the beautiful setting: the headwaters of a fabled river and the grove of trees that sheltered the encampment, enhancing it with bird life that included an eagle, which perched often on a tree overlooking the camp, a good omen. We told about the antelope that were in the area just beyond the camp, and that we had encountered rattlesnakes. At mention of rattlesnakes her immediate reaction was, "Did you kill them?" One of our group responded by saying that in the Indian world snakes are not adversaries, but are considered part of the natural web of life having their own place and function, and are respected; they are not killed, but are considered an integral part of animal life, which is honored in Indian ceremonies. The Hopi have a snake dance.

The people who made the statements to me about spirituality were representatives of a society that had lived successfully and productively on this continent for uncounted generations before Europeans arrived. They were deemed an impediment to "manifest destiny," which said providence had given Europeans the right and duty to subdue the continent and make it into their image. Indians were in the way and needed to be made into adversaries to justify removal: genocide, actually. The method was simple: make treaties, break them, turn Indians into adversaries when they resisted. That worked; Indian wars cleared the country and put the survivors on reservations. The Bureau of Indian Affairs controlled the reservations through an agent and set up local puppet governments. Over the years conditions have improved, but the essential facts remain: local governments, community services, social and political institutions were set up in our image, all alien to Native people. It would be like cutting the roots of a redwood tree thousands of years old, grafting a few new branches, and saying "now you are a pine tree, act like one." No roots, no life; existence only. Some adjusted, some didn't, and a great many were lost in the cracks between cultures, drifting with the current and using alcohol and drugs as sedatives; the worst of both worlds.

But the extraordinary leaders with whom I met at the headwaters were members of a group of die-hards, people to whom the heritage meant life itself. They had gone underground, keeping the spirituality, the ceremonies, the lifeways intact, guarding them with intense devotion and sense of responsibility much like medieval monks in what became Europe protecting their heritage, the flower of ancient civilization, from barbaric invaders. History repeated in the "New World": the same barbaric ignorance

of the wisdom and values of conquered people. I was to learn that each area of Indian country has its remnant group holding the wisdom of their ancestors, the spirit that has sustained countless generations and still sustains them. They are the traditional people who usually aren't visible and prominent, but they are there; strong in some areas, weak in others. They are the people with whom I have worked for the past 40 years, the people whose fingers are in the dike of disappearance and who need our help. They are the ones who in 1977 said to me, "We don't see any spirituality in your world," and, "We can help you."

Let me repeat some background for the impact of those statements. I was a musician, and left one of the best conducting positions on the east coast in the most culturally sophisticated area of the country: New England. I left because attendance at a Blood Indian camp in Canada during a summer break culminated years of interest in and attraction to Native American cultures. A new world opened, changing my life: a world of inclusion, a world where spirit prevails over struggle for material things, a world of respect for all life and all that supports it, a world of incredible freedom; a world that our forebears once inhabited but left behind for worlds filled with miracles of their creation, but in which the miracle of how all life is connected and our responsibility to it was lost.

I am a product of the world of our creation and was a participant in one of its highest achievements, classical music; music that opens spiritual windows to common humanity, common longing for connection to each other, and to forces beyond us. Connection that says the real power of the universe is love. The Beethoven 9th Symphony is considered a testament to universal brotherhood because of the choral text in the last movement, but all truly great

music does that. My orchestra was like a miniature UN with musicians from Asia, Europe, South America, Canada, and the United States. Men and women. Everyone focused on musical creation that took the best efforts of each and to which each was critical. Racism unthinkable, Chauvinism unthinkable, Violence unthinkable. Connection complete, and at its core, stripped of any triteness, was love; immense love that included not only those involved in re-creating great music but all of life in its magnificence. Everyone with the right heart emerges from those experiences changed a little; the long-term effect is compounding.

I left that life at its height to work with and for Native people; everyone thought I had taken leave of my senses, particularly my colleagues and my family. But they saw only the surface. My colleagues thought I was a little insane, running out on my gift.

From the time of European landfall, Indians have been a negative for many people or, at best, exotic curiosities. They were considered anachronistic, stuck in stone-age mentality and superstition. To be associated with them was considered not only intellectual suicide but economic and social suicide as well. These are attitudes that reflected abysmal ignorance of the one of the great peoples in the human family with rich cultures and deep spirituality. The journey that ended at the Missouri Headwaters meeting began during summer breaks when Ann and I returned to Montana from New England. I gravitated to Indian reservations. There are seven reservations in Montana and seldom do non-Indian Montanans go there to spend any time with the people except for celebrations such as Crow Fair. Montana is a huge state that could hold all of New England inside it, and to explore it requires a

lot of driving. I began to spend time in Indian Country and I had the good fortune of developing friendships with members of various Montana tribes, often bonding with people over a mutual love of horses.

The Native American history of Montana is a book that has never been written; public school students, at least in the days of my youth, had little exposure to either Indians or the stories of their age-old tenure in the West. It was almost as if history didn't begin prior to the first generation of white settlers arriving. Sure, we learned about Chief Joseph and the Nez Perce engaging in a battle with the U.S. Calvary and surrendering near the Bear Paw Mountains. And we visited what was then called the "Custer Battlefield" and were told of his annihilation even though it was Custer who started the fight and paid dearly for his error.

I could tell you about classical music from the Middle Ages to modern times. I could note how the Staffanson clan made its way from Scandinavia and ultimately arrived on the American "frontier." But I couldn't tell you, before experience with Indians began, anything about their cultures, oral traditions, and lifeways, nor of the richness of their cultures and the tragedy of their exile on reservations. When I was in school, it was almost as if we didn't want to know. And the underlying reason is that it would have complicated our own reason for being there.

As a Westerner who has roots in a region that only a short time prior to my birth had been the homeland of people whose identity had been shaped by the West in profound ways, something Dr. Martin Luther King, Jr. said during the days of the civil rights movement resonated with me and caused me to reflect on our cultural blind spot. King said, "History will have to record that the greatest tragedy of this period of social transition was not the strident clamor of the bad people, but the appalling silence of the good people."

In the late 1960s two Piegan Blackfoot friends, Nora and Willie Spanish, invited me to go with them to a Blood Indian Medicine Lodge summer encampment in which the nation holds its community religious and renewal ceremonies. Off the beaten path, the Bloods live for a time within their own cultural parameters, away from mainstream life.

Intrigued by the unexpected invitation from Willie and Nora, I accepted.

The Bloods (Kainai) are part of the Blackfoot Confederacy composed of Piegan Blackfoot who live in northwest Montana, Bloods who are just north of the Canadian border in Alberta, and the northern Blackfoot (Siksika) who are in Central Alberta.

Where I went with my Blackfoot friends is not, figuratively speaking, on any map. Topographically, the road to the Blood Camp wound through the high plains of Southern Alberta: grassland that had nurtured bison, elk, antelope, and legions of smaller animals and birds over endless years. Land that was framed on the west by the most imposing mountains on the continent, the Northern Rockies, glacier-filled and snow-covered, giving relief to the wide horizon of the prairie, and promising coolness and the mystery of deep forests; land that was home to human beings who had adapted to its rhythms and cycles over countless generations and who fit there as seamlessly as the bison, elk, and wolf.

157

The road took us through the heart of Blackfoot Country. I could not know that it was also a road of destiny. Take a road trip sometime with an Indian elder and what you'll hear are stories about events that happened on that landscape.

I could not imagine that this road's ending at a "medicine" encampment would open a window to me and that my future would be tied to what was on the other side. It existed in parallel and invisibly to the world we are taught to know.

Our vehicle stopped for inspection at the Canadian border, an international boundary on modern highway maps but which has no meaning for native people whose cultures knew only the natural geography. Their boundaries were those of the natural world that circumscribed the territory of the bison and other elements upon which their survival depended. Blackfoot culture once occupied a huge area stretching from what is now Alberta to as far south as southern Montana, its people moving freely within it, nomads trailing the seasons. The imposed international boundary was a nuisance, but had no relationship to their lives.

A border patrol agent came to our car. He was a young man who engaged in what he probably considered was friendly banter. "You Injuns better do your rain dance, it's been awfully dry here." In that casual comment he expressed an innate contempt for Indians. The term "Injun" was derisive. His reference to rain dance was like a knife in me. My companions remained calm and said nothing, probably immune, having been exposed to much worse denigration.

During those years, the national news media was filled with scenes from the civil rights movement's clashes in the deep South and it was always portrayed as Black/White. Native people have been mired in worse circumstances.

Noam Chomsky, the legendary linguist, civil rights crusader, and cognitive scientist at MIT, was born into an Ashkenazi Jewish family in Philadelphia. As a scholar, he comprehends profoundly the diabolical legacy of the Nazi Holocaust, and he has written that the Holocaust and attitude of genocide carried out against native peoples in the Americas is more evil in scale, scope, and duration.

The border agent waved us through. Eventually, after a considerable time on back roads, the Blood Camp came into view. Poles protruding through the tops of tipis with occasional short needle-covered branches became visible on the horizon, their dark geometric patterns set against white tipi covers, indicating the end of our journey.

The encampment had been set up at the same time of year going back beyond any tribal memory. It held a surviving group of a once dominant population. They were survivors in the sense that they clung tenaciously to values and ancient worldviews formed over countless generations; views which are spiritual at core; survivors in the sense that they withstood the onslaught of alien values and life-ways imposed by a society that considered indigenous cultures anachronistic and arrant. It took extraordinary integrity and courage to make the necessary outward adaption of walking the white man's road while keeping the internal, spiritual heritage intact. These survivors and my destiny were united by a spiritual hunger; a hunger fulfilled

by being together in this sacred space.

My anticipation of what I'd find, an expectation that had been building during the long trip from Montana, now became overwhelming. When my feet touched down, I stood in the midst of this huge encampment, its people moving about setting up the facilities. This was a time for them to remember, to dwell in each other's company at the most profound levels; to share ceremonies, many of which originated earlier, before the world changed with the invasion of Europeans.

I was the only non-native in camp. Willie, Nora, and I were guests of Frank Red Crow and Pat Weasel Head. Willie never said it, but I knew he had to receive clearance beforehand for me to enter.

The camp was composed of about 60 tipis, some with tents pitched behind, serving as kitchens. In the center was a large structure made of three overlapping tipis in which ceremonies involving large numbers of people were held. There were vehicles and many horses. The sight of many horses gave me a feeling of connection and common ground.

My friend Willie Spanish was my guide and advocate. He arranged my sleeping quarters and talked to me about the protocols of the camp.

I felt like a child in C. S. Lewis's *The Chronicles of Narnia* or Dorothy falling out of the sky into Oz. Everything was new; but strangely, I had a feeling of belonging, as if returning to a long forgotten childhood home.

It was as if I had been stripped of support built over the years and was again a young person among adults. Initially, I moved and spoke cautiously. Each day led me deeper into a world of spirit missing in my world.

My first evening was spent with Willie and others in

Pat Weasel Head's lodge. Hindsight tells me it was both an evening for Pat to meet with friends and to give me an introduction to the Blood Indian world. We ducked under the tipi entrance cover. The only light was a small fire burning in the center casting shadows and creating an atmosphere of serenity. Beds rolled up and covered with buffalo hide were placed around its circular edges. There were elk hide rugs. The tipi was spotlessly clean. There was formality in the evening; the guests and host were seated according to protocol. There was no chatter or loud conversation. No introductions were made on my behalf. It wasn't necessary. Everyone knew. I didn't know what to expect but I had a feeling of awe just sitting in the presence of these men, all of whom were a generation older than me. They reflected the calmness and authority of long tradition and experience. Their presence and manner expressed both respect and confidence.

Indian social events are never hurried. There is always time to adjust to the people and the occasion.

At the proper time Pat, seated on the right of the tipi entrance, welcomed his guests and began a story-telling evening. He told stories of his people before the world changed with the coming of Europeans. He had the story-telling skills and eloquence of traditional native people, who are inheritors of an oral culture and for whom it was, and is, their medium for entertainment and instruction. His delivery was part narration, part singing, and part pantomime. It held his audience spellbound. Since the narration was in the Blackfoot language, Willie often whispered to me, "I wish you could understand." No doubt that would have enriched the experience but its effect came through and touched me deeply.

I was reminded of an evening, in London, when I heard

the great Welch actor, Emlyn Williams, seated alone on an empty stage, reciting Dylan Thomas poetry. Hearing Pat without knowing his words, I felt the same "actor's spell" as with Emlyn William, in addition to the intimacy of an enhanced atmosphere. When the storytelling evening ended, the fire was low. Pat's eloquence had worked its magic. In a non-Indian setting there would have been congratulations and well-wishing. Not here. Too many words would spoil both the effect of the evening and the enhanced state of each guest. Leave-taking was quiet and respectful. Again, I did not understand the words which were in the Blackfoot language. There are no words to express the impact of being in the presence of people to whom, unknown to me at the time, the rest of my life would be dedicated.

Everything in Blood Camp revolved around aspects of creation and being thankful for what we are given in nature. The most important ceremonies took place in the Medicine Lodge. Some involved men's and women's societies, others included everyone. I moved about the camp freely but attended only the ceremonies to which I was invited. Adult activities consumed the days but nights were taken over by youth. After the evening meal, groups of young people on horseback would circle the camp counterclockwise, "schmoozing" and "showing off'" like all teenagers do.

I enjoyed watching them. A widow with her five-year-old boy occupied a tipi next to that of Pat Weasel Head; the boy bonded with me and talked about his life and his dreams of what he would do. He asked, "Where's your family?"

"They're not here," I said.

"I'll be your family," he answered, being unable to comprehend just how much the message resonated.

Slowly I let go of the protective layer each of us carries and saw a different worldview. Our society's first priority is material well-being with competition and individual achievement at its center. Our preoccupation is often with meaningless things tied to status. Too often spiritual life and concern for our footprint in the natural world are incidental or non-existent.

Traditional Native Americans reverse that order. The world of spirit is their first concern, animating both their lifestyle and their relationship to the natural world. For them, material well-being is the result of good spiritual practices. Competition in degree is present in any society, but for traditional people it is secondary to group welfare, The group comes first with its weakest elements receiving priority.

One evening I was sitting alone, writing, in Pat's tipi when he and a friend entered, saying nothing to me or each other. They sat on the earth floor on opposite sides of the fire, roasting strips of meat, cutting off with a knife bites that were held in the teeth; this was a scene that could have taken place centuries earlier. There was much of the old culture in camp. I remember two men seated in front of a tipi communicating in sign language. I remember waking up on a crisp morning when ground fog covered everything but the tops of tipis and hearing chants of the old ones out a distance from camp. I remember the drums. These expressions were not nostalgic indulgences, but manifestations of deep cultural values that define the people and reinforce the meaning of being native in a non-Indian world.

While I was introduced to friends of Nora and Willie, I was never asked about my reason to be there or my background. They accepted me through my friendship with the Spanishes and by being a guest of camp leaders Frank Red Crow and Pat Weasel Head. While I did not enter the large ceremonial tent, I saw some of its activities; one involved the Motokis, a women's society. A large number of women were outside the camp, bent over as if digging roots. Suddenly men on horseback burst out of the camp, surrounding them and driving them into the medicine tent. I couldn't follow them into the tent but the pageantry was exciting.

Beyond a general reference, I cannot and would not describe the ceremonies in more detail here, because any description or exposure sacrifices their meaning and destroys the bond of trust existing between participants and observers. That's why people do not take photographs or carry recorders.

One of Plains Indians' most sacred events is the transfer of a medicine pipe bundle from one owner to another. Medicine bundles are their most sanctified objects, some of which are very old, having been passed down from one owner to another for generations. Records of the origins and ownership of medicine bundles are carefully kept, giving them enhanced meaning and spiritual significance.

When Willie told me of our invitation to witness a bundle transfer ceremony that evening in the tipi of one of his friends, I was not fully aware of what an honor that

was. As he talked to me about medicine bundles, of their place and meaning in the culture of the people, I realized the privilege of the invitation; particularly to a non-Indian, very few of whom have witnessed it. The ceremony began in late afternoon in the tipi of the owner. The owner and his wife were seated at the back of the tipi. Ceremonial singers and drummers were on the right side with the medicine bundle, on a small table in the center. We were escorted to the left side, reserved for guests. The entrance of the young man to whom the bundle was being trans-ferred startled me. He was carried into the tipi on a hide supported by several men. He sat at the front of the tipi.

Since I did not know the language, I was not intruding on the sacred nature of the program; this was both my protection and what eased my conscience. But as with Pat Weasel Head's storytelling, the impact for me was intense. It is a long sequential ritual, each section followed by a time of relaxation in which participants talk and enjoy each other. Again any further description would be improper. Apart from their rightful place in Native American life, medicine bundles are both desecrated and meaningless if displayed in museums or written about; I can only describe the surface elements that made such a deep impression for me.

In some intervals of pause, the bundle owner's wife would harangue the group. Again, I did not understand her words but her agitation communicated. Those present paid little attention. Later Willie said she had told the group that my presence was creating a negative atmosphere which would ruin the ceremony.

Medicine bundles contain items of spiritual signifi-cance that differ with each bundle. This bundle contained a pipe associated with thunder and rain. During the cere-

mony, shortly after the pipe was taken out of its red flannel covering, rain suddenly occurred with such intensity that articles in the tipi "closet," the space between the tipi lining and cover, were taken out to keep them from getting wet. The owner of the bundle spoke to the group in an assuring way. Willie told me that he said, "You see, we are doing everything right; this is proof." My presence had not ruined the ceremony as his wife had suggested.

Around midnight, the ceremony ended. When we emerged outside I was shocked to see the wet ground extended only about ten feet. The downpour that had drenched the tipi didn't fit the realities of my world. There were no clouds, temperature changes, wind or moving fronts; no water source: no creek, no hoses. Camp water was brought in drums.

The ground under my feet seemed to have shifted. No one remarked about a phenomenon that to me was as preposterous as the sun suddenly changing direction. My mind reeled, but I didn't say anything; it was the climaxing experience within a reality as remote from mine as is Mars. A door had been opened to another world, a world of new and unknowable phenomena. My life would never be the same. The supernatural had entered my life in a dramatic way and would continue more deeply over the years, changing my concept of reality: a story I need to tell.

The supernatural is something our society avoids like a dream that doesn't make sense. We can't put it under the microscope of our senses and place it within the parameters of what we call the real world. It makes us uncomfortable because we are rationally sure it is hallucination; but there is the nagging suspicion: maybe it is not merely imagined. The drenched tipi was not caused by any human. The world is transformed in those moments

of transcendence and we are less sure that we are captains of our ship.

With the exception of the bundle owner who said the rain was a sign we were doing everything right, no Indian commented on a phenomenon that was staggering to me. I believe there were two reasons: first because the supernatural is an important part of their worldview, accepted as "normal" not exceptional, and second because it is unknowable. Talking about it or overanalyzing it weakens it, taking away the power of its impact. I thought of the border agent's remark, "You Injuns better do your rain dance," realizing that the gulf separating him from the people of the camp was not merely one of refinement or perspective, but was an entirely different spiritual universe; the gulf may be unbridgeable. I did not know then that the rest of my life would be devoted to helping indigenous people survive in their universe and to working against all odds to build a bridge between the two.

For me, classical music had been the epitome of spirituality; but it does not flaunt natural laws.

Weeks later I talked with traditional Indians outside the Plains tradition to determine whether the supernatural phenomenon I had witnessed relating to the medicine pipe fit a larger pattern. No one was surprised, and no one considered it an exceptional occurrence.

I don't recall the remainder of my time at the camp; its memory was blotted out by the impact of the bundle ceremony. I do vividly recall my departure. As I retraced the road traveled only a week earlier, I had a feeling of euphoria more intense than any experienced before or since.

When I returned to Ann, my countenance had changed. In retrospect I believe the euphoria was a transfiguration, a new awareness of the deep spiritual experience

of the camp. Her first question was, "What happened? You look different."

It took a while for me to reenter the world of summer activity before we packed up and returned to Springfield. I did not talk about the Blood Camp, but realized that my life had taken a turn and that it would involve the indigenous world somehow. Since I had no idea how that would happen, it was the source of some anxiety.

I come from a culture that demands explanations wrapped in logic for any happening outside the norm, and so I attempted to put my new experience in logical context; but the farther I waded into the meaning of the Blood Camp, the deeper the water became. I abandoned effort to reduce it to the pigeonholes of logic, and let its influence flow without restraint. A week's immersion is only a glimpse, I realized; but a glimpse, registered on an open psyche, can be transforming.

At the moment of Ann's question to me, unbeknown to her or me for that matter, the process of abandoning a successful and rewarding career in classical music had begun.

The most difficult decision of my life would take months; time to agonize over, to rationalize, to debate, to attempt to find an emotional and spiritual equilibrium that would clear a conscience pulled in opposite directions.

How could I, in an act that appeared impetuous to others, just run out on my profession? I had responsibilities to my colleagues in music, to those who supported its structure, to those who filled our concert hall, and to those young people beginning their journey in classical music.

How could I consider jumping off a rock-solid cliff unto an unknown void? The roots of the dilemma were deep. I had early experience with Indians, particularly riding with Blackfoot cowboys as a teenager and later

visiting with friends on a number of reservations; but I had no idea of working with them.

I had lived in the musical version of the sacred, expressed in one of its most intense forms: classical music. Music's abstract spirit had its own transforming effect on my life. The spirit of the indigenous world is not abstract; it encompasses all life and the elements that support life.

Consider: to the traditional indigenous mind, water has a form of "life" and traditional people cannot imagine pouring pollutants into it. The same applies to air, land, and all elements upon which life depends; all have sanctity. The people who hold these views are marginalized and called "primitive," "anachronistic," "passé." The larger society considers life other than human, and the elements that support life, to be utilitarian: unworthy of sanctity. Their acceptance of abuse and destruction of the natural world is dictated by profit and by the appetite of their economic engine to increasingly devour the world's resources beyond renewal, controlling people, not the reverse. These people are called "enlightened," "scientific," "modern," and "progressive." While the subtleties of the indigenous world evade pinning down, its contours are clear. The sense of community and the ease and comfort with which each person fits within it is, to me, unprecedented. The traditional native people are the least troubled and the most secure of any in my experience. They have kept materialism as a servant, not a master; the world of the spirit is their rudder and strength. Their world would be my preoccupation for the rest of my life.

I returned to my life in Springfield at the end of that summer, sensing that my life there was ending. The year was spent in processing what had happened and making the best possible conclusion to a career that had reached

the heights of a demanding profession. It was also a time for Ann and me to consider the ramifications of an abrupt change in life direction. The decision had to be made jointly. If Ann had objected or had felt serious misgivings about the new plans, they would have been dropped.

I want to emphasize Ann's courage here, her unselfish nature and magnanimity. She made my life work possible. With her love and support she enabled me to overcome difficult challenges. As I mentioned earlier, she grew up in Deer Lodge, Montana. We were kindred spirits. Her background as a pianist—in high school she won a state piano competition—her sensitivity to classical music, her outgoing personality, and prepossessing appearance allowed her to relate well to musicians and to excel in the social role incumbent upon the wife of a conductor. We were a team.

Few, if any, women would have willingly left that life for a new one in the West for only an idea, with an uncertain future. She truly had an understanding of the intense inner force that led me to leave a successful profession for the all-encompassing idea of addressing America's indefensible treatment of Native Americans. Mainstream society did not understand the rich cultures it bulldozed, relegating Native Americans to the bottom of human status and largely forgetting them.

Human beings are incomplete as individuals, needing a life partner for fulfillment. Ann and I have fulfilled each other to a degree we could not have anticipated. Our love has deepened decade after decade with road bumps handled through cooperation and kindness. Nearing the seventh decade it fills us to overflowing. Without that personal security the record outlined in this book could not have happened.

Leaving music created trauma, with physical ramifications, deeper than I had expected; but it was offset by

the challenge of addressing a problem as old as America.

I needed a period of decompression after leaving music. In the interim between leaving music and founding a new organization, I became Assistant Direct of what was then The Buffalo Bill Historical Center, which was later called The Buffalo Bill Center of the West in Cody, Wyoming. The Buffalo Bill Center is world renowned for its art collection and museums that celebrate the Old West. I wanted to assess that format as a potential means of creating cross-cultural communication.

While I was there, I contracted an illness that nearly cost me my life. I had rationalized the professional break from conducting intellectually and emotionally, but the message did not get through to my body. As a result of my struggling with the decision, I developed a kinked bowel that had severe ramifications: two surgeries and periodic stays in a hospital over six months. At one point Ann was told I had hours to live.

I want to pay tribute here to our daughter, Kristin, who is a joy to her mother and me and has deeply enhanced our lives beginning with an important role in saving my life. She was born during the depth of my illness from having left music: a miracle of new life, new promise, new hope. Her arrival gave my recovery greater urgency and provided a prescription no medication could match. She transformed the low point of my life into new heights, an important part of which took place during the early weeks of her life. While recuperating in bed, I would hold her and play with her most of the day. She would take naps lying on my chest, our hearts together. My recovery improved daily.

A Dine (Navaho) story says that White Shell Girl was the first Dine in human form. First Man found her on

a hill wrapped in a cloud beneath a rainbow drenched in dewdrops. Everything came to life when First Man found her. It was said that the colors of laughter, of light effervescence, traveled with her. She carried the promise of the people. Our newborn was our White Shell Girl and much came to life with her arrival. The color of love and fulfillment followed her. She carried the promise of our family; her miracle gave depth to my spirit.

Later, when we were in the difficult and uncertain atmosphere of establishing a new lifework, she was our anchor and our incentive. When she was old enough to ride horses I took her on trips into the Montana mountain wilderness. She became adept in riding and fit easily into the wilderness experience. Those were among the best times of our lives. When the Two Circles were formed—"Two Circles" is a generic name for the American Indian Institute and the Traditional Circle of Indian Elders—she was with her mother when they brought food to the first gathering of the Elders at the Missouri Headwaters. She adapted well to the new community of people, making friends there whose friendships have deepened over the years. She has had an important role in implementing our programs. Her function as my assistant in recent years has been critical for me as age takes its toll. She is my collaborator, confidant, and anchor of family love. She has been an indispensable part of the journey outlined in these pages. Her husband, Michael Campbell, and sons Bryan and Cody have contributed in many ways to the programs of the Two Circles, including help with both assembly and removal of facilities used in events and in transporting and assisting Elders Circle members. Kristin and Mike host Indian representatives on their visits to Bozeman.

During this time I lost much of my hearing from intensive doses of antibiotics taken over a long period of time. I remember the moment it started; my world closed in. It would limit me the rest of my life and deepen as age increased.

As a consequence, I, in middle age, was forced to develop lip-reading skills and adjustments of other kinds that made it possible to function. Beethoven became totally deaf in the prime of his career as a composer, but achieved his greatest work during that period. He was an inspiration for me to overcome that handicap. Classical music, however, was gone.

During our short time in Cody, plans for my work with traditional Indians began to take shape. While the museum format has potential for cross-cultural understanding, its scope did not fit my objectives. In 1971, Ann, Kristin, and I resettled in Montana's capital city, Helena, where we created the legal and functional structure of an organization as the next step toward implementing our ideas. We arrived in December of a cold and snowy Montana winter. Initially we moved into a family-owned cabin on Trout Creek some distance outside Helena. It was an idyllic winter setting. Occasionally we were snowed in. I worked daily on ideas for our new enterprise, driving to Helena often for consultation; but sometime every day I took our two-year-old daughter out on a sled, sometimes to slide down the slope against which the cabin had been built, sometimes taking her to see the deer that crowded our area. We built snowmen and played in the snow; at night I would toast marshmallows for her in the fireplace as we listened to the howls of coyotes. It was a therapeutic time for me.

A year later we formed the American Indian Institute. One of the founding trustees was Chet Huntley, retired NBC News anchor and founder of Big Sky Resort, a ski community near Bozeman. We moved to Bozeman to be near Chet Huntley and to assess Big Sky as a possible location for the Institute. The premise was that Big Sky would provide facilities for us as well as upkeep. However, it did not happen because our planning committee decided it would be inappropriate to be associated and identified with a commercial enterprise; but it had been tempting.

I was its professional staff, Ann the volunteer. She was the telephone voice for the new enterprise, greeting Indian and non-Indian callers alike with her warm response and understanding in the face of all kinds of questions. I had considerable earlier contact with Native Americans; she had none. But over the years she has fit in with native people as well as she did with musicians in New England. I am indeed fortunate that the love of my life has been my best work partner.

The motive was driven by a realization in Canada that the richness of indigenous cultures was not only unknown in the outside world, but also that their oppression was fed by stereotype and caricature. So much was lost in translation between parallel worlds. Communication across cultures based on reality, not stereotype, was needed. That, I thought, should be the mission of the American Indian Institute.

I set out to build a new coalition of native and non-native people, free of organizational bureaucracy and based on a structure fitting Native American worldviews rather than corporate hierarchy. After working up the legal charter of the American Indian Institute, the nascent work of defining its functions began and would take considerable

time, involving meetings with native and non-native people around the country. Skepticism abounded. Fortunately, I found excellent help in Indian Country. Alfonso Ortiz, Tewa anthropologist, and D'Arcy McNickle, Salish anthropologist, activist, and creator of the Center for the History of the American Indian at Chicago's Newberry Library, became my colleagues in the planning process. Basically, the idea was that the institute would function as a clearinghouse communication center that would share the authentic native voice with other native and also non-native people.

No one thought it would work.

In my first contact with Barney Old Coyote, who headed the Indian studies department at Montana State University, he looked at me quizzically. With a sigh, indicating his skepticism, he handed me a small publication listing the myriad organizations dedicated to "helping" Native Americans; all these groups allegedly were committed to bettering conditions for Indians, and almost all of them had been short lived. The implication of his response was that our organization would be redundant and unlikely to receive support, since we didn't have a formula to address the "problem."

Our approach was to work with Indians in determining a formula for our work. That was new.

A number of academicians supported our idea; however, they were also skeptical of adding another organization to those others already existing that had good intentions but were often negative for Indians, souring them on mainstream help.

In an era of tight money, funding was an issue. Lloyd Kiva New, co-founder of the Institute of American Indian Arts in Santa Fe, asked, "Do you think the heavens are

going to open up and shower the money to create this big project?"

It was not a promising picture, but no one was doing what we wanted to do and I was determined. Since I was the only staff, I realized it would take time.

This was a time when all minorities were getting more attention and political clout; but misunderstanding, outright hostility, and stress dominated.

Through the regional Bureau of Indian Affairs, I arranged a meeting with the Montana Intertribal Policy Board in Billings. I didn't expect help but I wanted them to know about our plans. When I arrived the bureau director said, "I don't think you should go in there; they're laying for you."

I spoke briefly about our new organization and asked for questions. The chairman drew himself up like Cochise facing an army courier, and dripping with sarcasm said, "What makes you think you can be in the Indian business?"

The Indian business? The conversation went downhill from there. Barney Old Coyote, Crow, was my only friend in the group. I felt a little like Custer except that I escaped.

Considerable opposition came from political Indians and Indian activists, which I understood.

The idea of some white guy telling Indians he intended to work with them in getting their voice across cultures was a red flag. First of all I was a meddler, and I had to have a nefarious motive. Second, providing assistance was something only Indians should be involved in and tying it to a white organization was the height of disrespect. Antagonism toward our work from activists continued for many years.

Opposition also came from mainstream social service

groups and non-profit organizations who thought I was trying to usurp their "territory." Others thought I had gone off the deep end by working with Indians. I lost many friends; it wasn't that I was avoided, but there was a chill in the relationships. Being associated with Indian people other than trying to make them into our image had always carried disparaging consequences and labels. If Indians knew what was good for them, the story goes, they would just move on and assimilate into "the dominant culture."

Indeed, the American Indian Movement (AIM) had been the very public front for activism. Various events made national headlines: the occupation of Alcatraz, the march on Washington, D.C., and the Wounded Knee confrontation were prominent events, but the response often was to deepen feelings of racism. Some people welcomed the emergence of minorities from under the heel of the larger society; however, there was a backlash among its institutions, making it difficult for us to find support.

"You must be distressed by the actions of AIM," the president of Springfield College, Bill Locklin, said to me. The implication was that the disruption of the status quo would cripple our effort. The tactics of AIM were not my tactics, but I recognized them as a pincers movement to pierce the implacable armor of racism, and that they were necessary to get the attention of society. Forty years later that climate has improved, but racism is still strong. It will take generations of enlightenment to eliminate it.

Fortunately there were people and institutions in our early years who were willing to support our modest planning budget. The final planning seminar was held at "Wingspread" in Racine, Wisconsin, the Frank Lloyd Wright home that the Johnson Foundation had turned

into a conference center. The nine delegates included Indians from the United States and Canada, a representative of the Carnegie Corporation, an associate of the renowned California designer Charles Eames, and me.

Our plan to create a communications center for traditional Native people was thoroughly discussed. Two statements clarified our approach. Oren Lyons, a member of the Council of Chiefs of the Onondaga Nation, was a new participant.

"I don't see any of my people here," he said, meaning grass-roots traditional people. Alfonso Ortiz said, "If what we want to do doesn't make sense to the Elders, it won't work."

We decided to call a meeting of grass-roots traditional leaders from across North America. Each Indian delegate would contact the most respected traditional leaders in their area. I would contact Montana traditional Indian leaders. The result was an August 1977 convening of thirty-five traditional leaders from the four directions in North America, at the headwaters of the Missouri River in Montana.

The Missouri Headwaters was chosen for its symbolism and as a possible site for the American Indian Institute's communication center. The headwaters had been an Indian gathering place for millennia. A chert mine (for arrow and spear points) at the site was carbon-dated to 800 A.D. A "pishkun" (buffalo jump) was only a few miles away. The area had been used by many tribes but was not "home country" to any. It symbolized joint use, and the joining of three rivers to form the Missouri symbolized beginning and promise. The area where the Elders would meet on the west bank of the Headwaters could be a consecrated site for Indian use only. The east bank area could be the

site of the American Indian Institute communication center. Communication could originate in the Indian sector and be processed and distributed in the non-Indian sector, separated both symbolically and physically by the river: this would be the location of Two Circles.

The Headwaters proved to be an auspicious setting. The tipi camp was isolated in a natural setting that included wildlife. An eagle often perched in trees over-looking the camp. Antelope frequented the area. Upon arrival, a delegate from Onondaga cast a fishing line into the river, catching a large trout. Montana weather proved its eccentricity with a late August snowstorm. Coats and storm gear were provided for five Hopi delegates and others from warm climates not used to winter in August. As an indication of the national paranoia regarding minority activities, a surveillance plane circled the camp for a time each morning.

For a number of years we were aware of federal agents monitoring our meetings in both urban and rural settings. We often had meetings in a Santa Fe, New Mexico hotel. Upon leaving we would see federal agents seated in the lobby; Oren Lyons would acknowledge them, letting them know we were aware of their presence. They never smiled. Since our meetings were not publicized, they may have learned about it from the hotel. That also happened in other cities. For a number of years, police cars would patrol our council camps, some of which were on remote reser-vations. I have no idea how they found us in remote places, but possibly it was from informants in the political Indian community. They never interfered with us, though we had a constant feeling of harassment.

The thirty-five traditional leaders at the Missouri Headwaters were themselves deeply skeptical. What hap-

pened there was unprecedented. On the one hand they had never been invited to come together in their environment on their terms to talk about better communication with the larger world, and without a pre-conceived agenda usually rigged against them. Also they were meeting with one non-Indian, not a battery of people symbolizing power and coercion. They were intrigued.

On the other hand a history of disappointment in cross-cultural meetings fueled their suspicion. The Crows were official hosts since this was territory in which they had hunted for generations. We sat on cottonwood logs around a fire that had been lit in ceremonial preparation for the meeting. As an indication of the skepticism, Phillip Deere, Muscogee from Oklahoma, put a small tape recorder on the ground near where I was sitting, placing it with a flourish which indicated doubt.

The Crows, led by Tom Yellowtail, welcomed the group. There were introductory conversations common to all traditional meetings. Oren Lyons, Onondaga, who had been present in the Wingspread planning meeting, spoke first about our idea of developing a communications center to bring understanding of Native people to the larger world through the unfiltered words of traditional leaders.

He suggested that the area of the camp might be consecrated as a spiritual site for use by Indians only, noting that there was no ecumenical site not associated with a particular nation. He talked about a clearinghouse for the traditional voice, operated by the American Indian Institute on the opposite river bank to bring messages from traditional people to the larger society. I followed with suggestions of how the joint enterprise might function and explained that the American Indian Institute would be the support source and administrative agency for the Two

Circles. Traditional native people don't hurry a discussion, beginning immediately with pros and cons. They allow new information to simmer, meanwhile talking of other things.

No one before had offered them a hand on their terms with no strings attached, and they were sure there had to be a hook somewhere. They liked the idea of a spiritual site connection to a communications center on their terms, but they had to be convinced of the sincerity of the offer and that it involved no ulterior motives. That would take time. Actions, not words, would remove doubt and create a climate for cooperation. It took several years to convince them there was no ulterior motive and to gain their complete trust.

Here, I want to express my respect and friendship for Oren Lyons, who today is known worldwide for his advocacy on behalf of indigenous rights. A charismatic speaker, he has appeared in venues around the world and in the United Nations as de facto spokesperson for millions of indigenous peoples in their struggle against racism, broken treaty rights, loss of homelands, and marginalization. Oren is an ardent environmentalist because it is central to his being and in the worldview of his people.

Born in 1930, he is a member of the Council of Chiefs of the Onondaga Nation and a recognized scholar on treaties and the interaction of the early colonists with indigenous populations. Multi-talented, he is a fine artist and a renowned athlete, an all-American lacrosse player at Syracuse University and one of the founders of the Iroquois Nationals, a lacrosse program representing the Six Nations Iroquois Confederacy in international competition. He's been featured in documentaries, including one hosted and produced by Bill Moyers, and he appeared

in the critically acclaimed documentary "The 11th Hour."

A strong voice in the Traditional Circle of Indian Elders and Youth, Oren and I became close friends. He carries his Nation's message of Indigenous Peoples' rights, peace, and environmental responsibility around the world. He said, "At first I wanted to defend the Iroquois. Then my sights broadened to embrace other Indians. Then I saw this had to include defending indigenous peoples all around the world." He is one of the most prominent voices on behalf of indigenous peoples in the world today.

Oren also said about the work of the Two Circles, "Because of Two Circles, different tribes are communicating with each other in ways that didn't happen for 500 years. And we're talking with our brothers and sisters in Africa and Asia and people in the north of Scandinavia and Russia and the South Seas. Bob Staffanson knew that we have an important perspective to offer the world. It isn't political wisdom. It rises up out of the ground. Our wisdom is based upon respect for the Earth and offering thanks for enabling us to survive."

The gathering at the Missouri Headwaters was the first test of our working cooperatively with traditional Native Americans, on their terms, to address centuries of cultural and spiritual genocide. At that point, and during the defining years, no one, Indian or non-Indian, thought it would work. Some on both sides were hopeful; but all the odds, historical and current, pointed to failure. No one was more aware of the odds than I, but the first gathering gave me hope. The most respected traditional leaders had come together at our invitation, had listened to me and to each other and however deep the skepticism, had agreed to continue the discussion. It was up to our side to prove our good faith. That would take time; but the

outcome of the first Elders meeting was an unprecedented foundation on which we could build our new program. I no longer had any doubts.

The depth of antagonism to our work from political Indian activists and mainstream sources was apparent early, but the most unexpected and disturbing effect of my entering the racial arena was feeling the depth of animosity and hate within the informed and educated elements of society from whom I expected prejudice, but not outright hostility.

Perhaps the most blatant example of hostility happened when George O'Connor, our board chairman, and I were scheduled to give a presentation for our new enterprise at a convention of bankers in Calgary. We needed financial support. O'Connor, Chairman of Montana Power Company, was deeply respected in the business community. I spoke first, making a case for supporting indigenous cultures and traditions. There was no reaction.

After George spoke and asked for questions the reaction was immediate. He was humiliated by the group, as it behaved in an unexpectedly juvenile way. They made fun of him, calling him Pollyanna, and ridiculing him in a way that shocked me. I was not worthy of their ridicule but George, a colleague, received the brunt of their sarcasm. It was another wake-up call. There was no mention or discussion of our program, just racially-driven derision.

No doubt alcohol contributed to the breaching of courtesy and to the recitation of how Indians were beneath contempt, each one trying to top the others with derogatory stories. We got no support, but did receive a lesson in hatred and resentment of Indians. To George's credit, his treatment did not diminish his interest and support of our work. We left a hostile atmosphere, which I was to

experience again and again in the years ahead, usually with less direct mean spiritedness.

A few of our personal friends were interested in our new endeavor, but when inquired about it at a social gathering, some people left, offering comments like, "It's better than having to hear about Indians." I approached many Montana business leaders for help as the Two Circles was getting underway. Three or four supported us modestly, led by Montana Power Company and Big Sky Resort; others simply dismissed us when the word Indian was mentioned. On one occasion we were setting up a council camp at Austin Two Moons' place on the Northern Cheyenne reservation. At the end of the day two Indians went with me to a Hardin, Montana bank to cash a check and get supplies. We were in work clothes and the teller looked at us as if we were vermin, telling us to wait on chairs in a corner. In the meantime he waited on a number of other people. Finally he summoned me and said, "We can't cash this check until it clears to us," which would take days. The Institute's check was issued by a bank in Bozeman and cashing it could have been authorized with a single phone call. But because I was in the company of native people, he hassled me.

My arguing and pleading made no difference until I told him that George O'Connor was part owner of the bank and I would call him. Reluctantly, the teller cashed the check. Almost at every turn we were given the brush-off when the word "Indian" was mentioned. Mainstream foundations would have nothing to do with us in the beginning. Left-leaning foundations, the most likely source, would not support us because their grant would not go directly to Indians but to a third party. We survived in the early years by contacts and doors opened by our trustees

O'Connor, Tim Babcock, Meri Jaye, and Joe McDowell, as well as contributions from the trustees, most importantly Mrs. Meri Jaye in San Francisco. Indispensable help, both financial and supportive, came from Ann Roberts, Margot and Roger Milliken, Grant Abert, and the Threshold Foundation.

As mentioned earlier, the first day of the Headwaters gathering closed with this admonition directed to me: "We don't see any spirituality in your world. We don't see any spirituality in your government, your commerce, your education, your religion."

This statement was made to educate me and establish parameters for our relationship. They were telling me that while I was offering help to them they believed that we needed help, that our materialistic society lacked core values to sustain equitable and compassionate human relationships and a balanced use of natural resources, and that they could help us. The quotient of help would be a two-way street. That proved true to a degree that I could not then imagine. The first meetings were unprecedented in creating a process that resulted in a trust relationship and cooperative undertaking that was new in the history of Indian/non-Indian relationships.

At the close of the Headwaters meeting Oren Lyons asked the group, "Do we want to have another meeting?" Their positive response meant they wanted to consider these radically new ideas further, confirming the birth of a new cross-cultural relationship. That it took a half dozen years to completely formulate the relationship between the Two Circles, and more to reach maturity, meant we were on "Indian time," a derisive term for most non-Indians but a quality trait in the minds of traditional Native Americans. American society is geared to instant gratification:

in terms of building a new organization it means months for a basic structure, not years. I entered with my society's sense of time, telling Indian planners that I had operating money for three years and by that time we should have developed a structure, programs, and fundraising to a point of being independent. The response was one of smiles, behind which was implied, "He has a lot to learn."

Among the things I did learn quickly was to slow the pace down and let things happen in due course without pushing. I learned patience and persistence. I already had persistence built in but Indians taught me patience, a great gift. We were not forcing change but creating conditions for it to happen. One of those conditions was time to allow new ideas to root deeply in the consciousness of the people involved, and in that process, to develop leaders and implementers to meet the challenges ahead. Since I was alone with Indians during much of the planning process, in a sense I became one of them, absorbing new qualities of thinking and new values. That learning has continued more than forty years, making me a different person from the one who called the Headwaters meeting.

While the original idea of a "communications center" was not abandoned, a new focus developed around the need for an ecumenical coalition of traditional leadership that would become known as the Traditional Circle of Indian Elders. Historically, meetings of traditional leaders of various Indian nations were common in Pre-Columbian times, but had been interrupted with the advent of Europeans in America.

Thereafter Indian ecumenical meetings became political, involving leadership both within and outside the Bureau of Indian Affairs system. Traditional leadership remained largely underground, although there had been

short-lived attempts to bring it back through efforts such as the 1967 "Unity Caravan," when Hopi and Iroquois Confederacy Nation Elders and others traveled from reservation to reservation breathing new life into the traditional fires that were near to flickering out. Elders at the Headwaters saw this as an opportunity to build a coalition of traditional leaders throughout North America, renewing an ancient tradition. It would be a Spiritual Circle in the ancient tradition rather than a modern political coalition. Its concern would be the spiritual underpinning which had sustained their people for millennia and which was threatened more deeply each year by the larger society's economic engine, which served material well-being first with little concern for environmental damage or the debasement of marginalized people who didn't fit its credo. Because there was a commitment of no-strings support from the American Indian Institute, traditional leaders, who had little financial backing, would be spared the financial burden of finding funds for their gatherings. The idea of making the headwaters a permanent site for traditional gatherings was abandoned for a plan to move them each year to a different part of Indian country in North America, in order to reach Elders who do not travel.

Over the next four "councils" held at Hopi in Arizona, Phillip Deer's roundhouse in Oklahoma, Cree country in northern Alberta, and at Onondaga in New York State, the details of a working relationship between the American Indian Institute and the growing coalition of traditional Elders from Indian country in North America was developed. The effort would be structured in the Indian way: two "Circles," one Indian and one non-Indian, held together not by signed agreements but by mutual trust. The Indian Circle would have no signup sheets, no hier-

archy. The members would know "where they sit" by an unstated internal process evolved over time. It would be a spiritual circle open to any Indian except those who would use it for personal or tribal agendas, whose objectives were at odds with the cultural/spiritual focus of the Circle, or who were advocates of other organizations; they would not be dismissed, but because of a lack of response to their agendas together with a negative comfort level, they would eliminate themselves. That worked. The American Indian Institute (the non-Indian Circle) would hold the mainstream 501c3 status connection and would be the support source and administrative agency for Two Circles enterprises. The Two Circles would be autonomous and not mixed.

Two goals emerged: First, the non-Indian Circle would support the Elders in efforts to sustain their heritage, their cultures, and values systems with no strings attached; second, there would be a joint effort to project the authentic Native American voice across cultures. That voice would also be added, where appropriate, to domestic and international dialogue on major issues confronting humankind. No politics would enter and funding would come from private sources, not government. Programs would be determined jointly and would be limited to cultural and spiritual issues. We would not "raise our flag," i.e., promote the Two Circles in the media; we wanted to avoid attracting "wannabes" or those who would use the Circles personally. Elders' Circle participation would be built by word-of-mouth. Based on agreement of the nature of programs, both sides would stay within those parameters and the honor of both Circles would be upheld by its members.

The Elders took a "long view," knowing the implaca-

ble obstacles ahead. They said that until what we wanted to do has passed through a couple of generations it could not be fully evaluated, needing the stamp of several generations to prove its worth and establish its ongoing effect. The vision was to attack major issues at root level rather than focusing on band-aid solutions that provided temporary relief, but little to fix root causes. It was a courageous vision. This was the first time a coalition of traditional leaders representing the four directions had been organized on their terms with a "Brothers Circle" to provide assistance, cooperation, and long-term organizational underpinning. The Elders Circle became the de facto leadership group for traditional Native Americans and the American Indian Institute became its clearinghouse. The impact of the Two Circles has been deep in North America and around the world.

Human beings need contact with like-minded people to achieve challenging goals; the Traditional Circle provides that contact by renewing the ancient custom of joint council. Each year The Circle gathers in a different area of Indian Country in North America to meet with traditional people concerned about sustaining cultural and spiritual heritage. The Elders do not bring a blueprint for cultural renewal, but bring their wisdom to draw out that of the host group. They don't come as teachers but as friends; they leave as colleagues on a mission. The local people would have to address the problems in their way; the Circle lit the fire. It produced dramatic results. We would hear of long abandoned ceremonies being renewed, of new longhouses or medicine lodges, programs for children, language revival; cultural pride and integrity became central again as well as an optimistic outlook. New life. Those results were deepest in areas where the heritage had thinned, but

even in areas where it had remained strong the Circle provided a renewing and energizing effect.

The Two Circles gained the support of the best Indian legal minds who are working in the very contentious arena of attaining justice in the wake of broken treaties, violations of property and water rights, royalty payments, first amendment issues involving free speech and protection of language, and the archaeological pilfering involving human remains and artifacts that are housed in prominent museums. They are on the front lines of legal engagement while the Traditional Circle of Elders works to hold the cultures together.

The late Tonya Gonnela Frichner, founder of the American Indian Law Alliance with offices in New York City and New Mexico, penned a note to the Institute and shared this observation. "For many years, the American Indian Law Alliance, in fulfilling our mandate of support to the traditional leadership of our Native American nations, has looked to the Circle for inspiration, guidance, and direction.

"We have always believed that the wisdom of our elders, passed onto our youth, through generations of struggle, has been the single most important factor in our continued survival against such overwhelming odds. The maintenance of our traditions, through the memory of our elders, preserves our traditional cultures and the critical components of our oral history. The gatherings of the Circle reflect our ancient values and provide our leaders with a forum in which to discuss issues critical to our beliefs as peoples and share their vision of a future with us. The Circle is a source of strength, a unique resource and an invaluable tool in the preservation of our way of life; a way of life that is critical to the maintenance of

balance in a world that more than ever needs the insight of Indigenous wisdom."

The commonalities of Native American outlook and the degree of cohesion among all nations, despite wide separation, was a shock to me. A gathering of the Elders Circle in a small village in Northern Alberta, Canada Cree country near the Northwest Territories border, included 50 delegates from the United States along with a delegation of Maya from Guatemala and 50 delegates from Canada including the host group, some of whom had never left their territory and spoke only their own language. The arriving guests were not asked about their purpose in meeting there; the question they received was, "What took you so long?" It was a reunion of friends even though they had never seen each other.

This was our first council in the far north. During a preliminary visit in early summer the sun set for a time but light continued. At midnight a paper could be read without light and people were still active outdoors. The council occurred in early fall with sunlight limited. Meetings were held in a large open area flanked on one side by arctic brush and timber, the large council space circumscribed by small poles planted in the ground outlining its circumference. Evening dances were held there, the darkness overcome by a huge fire casting its flickering light and shadows, creating an exotic atmosphere for dancers and leaving lasting impressions. Drums and dancing are the common elements that draw all Native Americans together and in the presence of which there is no division or discord.

I believe this is universal among indigenous people. In her book *Out of Africa*, Karen Dinesen Blixen notes an exception. At a large Kikuyu dance in Kenya involving hundreds of people, a group of Maasai appeared uninvited. Kikuyu and Maasai were traditional enemies. The Maasai were received cordially and were given seating but the atmosphere changed, becoming charged. Dancing became faster and more intense. Shortly after, a commotion occurred in which a Kikuyu was killed, ending the dance. The author's opinion was that the Maasai came to compete as dancers to show off their skills rather than to make trouble; but hot tempers intervened, ending what could have been a classic competition of expert dancers. The drum and dancing are magnets for all indigenous people.

As darkness increased in our northern setting, the dancers moved closer to the fire, creating striking shadows and silhouettes. At intervals between dances the hosts distributed food. Tipis were pitched nearby; as I walked past one of them I heard a voice inviting me inside. Louie Bad Wound, Oglala Sioux, a good friend, was visiting a host and eating a grouse which had been prepared over the tipi fire. I sat with them, sharing the grouse which tasted better than any restaurant food. I talked at length with a Cree trapper who runs a line deep in the Alberta wilderness. He uses a dog team to run the line and digs a hole in the snow under a big spruce tree for his night camp. A fire in his shelter keeps him warm even at 40 and 50 degrees below zero. He feeds his dogs wheat, which he boils for them making a kind of mush.

We learned much from a group of aged Cree elders who spoke with candor and eloquence about the life of their people and their place in the natural order of their environment and in the community of human beings.

Daily council sessions took place in an open area. A ceremonial fire burned in the center with chairs for participants around it.

There was three-way interpretation for speakers: English, Cree, and Spanish. At first I thought this would be burdensome but it worked well. Indian conferences are not agenda and time driven, creating a relaxed and congenial atmosphere which allowed time to absorb the thoughts of the previous speaker while the interpretations were underway.

Midway into the week a startling event occurred. Birds migrate early from northern regions and all had left except ravens and hawks. At one point in a morning meeting of the Circle, a small grey bird suddenly appeared at Leon Shenandoah's feet. Leon was principal Chief of the Iroquois Confederacy. It bobbed its head, climbing up on Leon's shoe and standing there for a moment, then hopped off and went to the person sitting on his right where it jumped up on *his* shoe, again remaining for a time and looking around. Everyone was aware of the bird but no one acknowledged it.

Discussion continued with no reference to the bird's presence. It continued its journey around the Circle stopping and perching on the boot or shoe of each person. One of the Elders took a paper cup, cut it in half and placed the lower half filled with water in the path of the bird. It was a symbolic gesture, the only acknowledgment of what to me was an unbelievable happening; to the others, it was unusual but not an aberration in their world. Children had become aware of the bird; some of them tried to get through the Circle but were stopped. The bird completed its journey around the Circle, stopping in front of Leon where it disappeared. Only then did the group stop to acknowledge the presence of the bird, not with excited reaction but with a calmness that reflected acceptance of a deep but not exceptional spiritual experience.

They did not discuss what it might mean, but they did talk of what its source might be among those they call upon. I cannot speak for them regarding their understanding of the bird's mission but I can say that it had a benign effect. A respectful group became more respectful, more cohesive and more one family. A group that had been welcomed as friends by their hosts now became something deeper. They were bonded beyond any human action or ceremony. I was shaken but my response was tempered by the calmness of the group. It was my good fortune to be a witness and to share the bonding.

I wrote earlier about a similar messenger that came to me at my home. Walking in my yard in early evening, I saw a grey bird somewhat larger than a robin flying low toward me; expecting to be dive-bombed, I stopped. Instead it landed on my head! I can still feel its talons sinking through my hair. Since I am not a tree, I considered the bird deranged, and attempted to shake it off; it didn't move, but dug its talons deeper. When I lifted it from my head it looked at me without struggle. I held it in the flat of my hand so that it could fly away; but it remained, looking at me. Mystified, I put it on my shoulder where it stayed until I reach our patio. When I put it down on the grass it flew into the bushes.

Considering the episode to be an anomaly but nothing more, I forgot about it. The next morning the bird was perched on the back of our couch. Realizing this was no normal bird, I picked it up. This time it looked at me with energy streaming from its piercing red eyes, its bill rapidly flapping. I held it for some time, mesmerized. When the

bill stopped I spoke to it, thanking it for coming, then taking it outside and placing it down in the same spot as before. This time it did not fly away: it vanished. Shaken, I had no idea how to think about what had happened. There was no context I could imagine, no parameters for logical thought. It was real (my wife was a witness) but it defied our concept of reality. I didn't talk about it to local friends, but I did call several Indian friends who were not surprised but impressed. They had no insight regarding its origin or meaning except those they may have kept to themselves, since I was still new in their association.

Our society has no tools for understanding the reality of the bird's visit to me. In spite of the outstanding achievements of science, we are vastly more ignorant than knowledgeable about cosmic reality, and our minds are closed to incidents such as I experienced. Later in my work with traditional Native Americans, I found similar paranormal events to be commonplace. Such events are accepted and integrated into their lives without any questioning, no doubt because these phenomena are in their heritage and accepted as "normal" and helpful without the need to be dissected. They are accepted in the same way the mysteries of life and the natural world are accepted. It's part of their ability to fit "inside" the natural world and not apart from it, as happens in our society. I respect science deeply, and am alive because of recent scientific discoveries; but I believe that science is also a source of arrogance on the part of many in "advanced societies," creating a sense of omnipotence that denigrates phenomena outside of their known parameters.

The bird's visit to me was a pivotal point in my learning curve. I had seen paranormal events before but always in association with Indians. This was the first time it hap-

pened to me directly and in a very dramatic way. I crossed a rare threshold. The world of spirit opened to me in ways that I could not have imagined. It was tangible evidence that there are other dimensions that can impact our society. Our society, having been disconnected from those dimensions, loses track of important realities. Indians helped me connect with that world. This experience has also made me realize that science does not have the last word regarding cosmic realities.

Another example of the different realities traditional Native Americans experience took place in 2013 when José Lucero, Tewa, honored us with a three-day visit.

On the second day of his visit, José expressed a desire to return to the Flying D Bison Ranch owned by Ted Turner, where we had held our 25th anniversary gathering of the Traditional Circle.

The Flying D, acquired by Turner in 1989, was a cattle ranch, its more than 119,000 acres situated between the Gallatin and Madison rivers in strikingly beautiful country bordering the Spanish Peaks Wilderness in Montana. Turner turned it into bison range, holding between three and four thousand head in addition to elk, moose, deer, bear, and wolves in substantial numbers. At the 2000 gathering, Joe Medicine Crow gave Turner his great-grandfather's name, "Buffalo Bull Chief."

José and I journeyed out to visit the bison early on a clear, cool, beautiful morning. As if we were expected, the herd was on lower Spanish Creek on both sides of a county road running through part of the ranch. Countless bison were on surrounding hillsides and up a connecting valley as far as the eye could see. We drove slowly, stopping to see the play of spring calves and the action of an undisturbed herd. At an appropriate place we stopped, left the

car, and stood, motionless, watching the animals. Our presence was accepted. After a time I returned to sit in the car. José sang the Pueblo buffalo honoring song and I watched in awe as at least thirty cows and calves made a semi-circle around José, watching him and listening.

Legend says that in the beginning, animals and humans could talk together. They still can do that, although discourse is not in words but in language of the spirit: direct spirit-to-spirit communication. Science would call it "telepathy": communication through means other than the senses. Animals and young children have it, but we lose it as we become more sophisticated and dependent upon language. Some, however, retain it; to do so, human beings must be open, humble, and accepting in mind and spirit. I saw communication taking place so deeply that day that wild animals came together around José.

I can say that I returned drained of emotion but with an energized spirit that stays with me today. I can also say that at my age, the encounter had more meaning in the context of the years I have spent learning about native lifeways than it would have had earlier in my life; and it has deepened my respect and affection for all indigenous peoples.

My life both before and after association with traditional Native Americans has been deeply influenced by forces I do not understand. I acknowledge them with gratitude and accept them now without the need to understand. I believe the bird communicated to my subconscious mind by the same method that allowed it to enter the house without openings, but I have no idea how that could happen; more important is that I have no need to understand how it could happen. For many reasons the bird's visit remains special; I held something from another dimension in my hand.

While hindsight tells me that paranormal and super-natural forces were impacting me prior to association with traditional Native Americans, it was not until I entered their world that those forces became clear to me through my own experience and observation. There was nothing of that nature in the culture of my youth. Years in classical music enhanced spiritual growth; but association with traditional Native Americans provided new form and substance.

My experience with the bird that entered my house when all entrances were closed was the climax of many contacts with paranormal events over a lifetime: all were outside the purview of science. I have felt a "wind at my back," a sense that I am not alone in life's journey. In facing seemingly impossible odds I have felt security, calm-ness, and lack of intimidation that goes beyond rational thought. Several instances are noted in these pages; one of the most dramatic was the lack of nervousness, appre-hension, or tension when I walked up to the podium to conduct the Philadelphia Orchestra before an auditorium filled with critics, even though I had no experience beyond a couple years with a community orchestra.

Sometimes these events occur at a superficial level. On a bright sunny morning in an Elders Circle camp on a remote area of the Pima reservation south of Phoenix, Arizona, I drove into the city to get supplies. On the return trip I noticed a heavy dark cloud over the area of the camp, but thought nothing of it. The sky was clear when I turned off pavement onto a dirt road leading to the camp. As soon as my front wheels left the pavement I knew it was a mistake because they sank deep into the muddy road. Because I could not back up, the only option was to try keeping the car on the road during the mile-long trip

to the camp. The car often slipped sideways, sometimes becoming partially stuck. I inched my way, and was relieved to finally see the cookhouse at the entrance to our camp. As I turned in I noticed with a sinking feeling that the camp was empty. Everyone had been evacuated to dry quarters. I was at an impasse. There was no way I would attempt to drive back to pavement; it was late and I would likely end up stuck or in the ditch with no one to help: not a pleasant prospect. I became resigned to spending the night in my car. I needed to be at the Phoenix airport early the next morning to meet incoming participants. That was out.

While all of this was going through my mind, a very large white truck turned into the camp entrance. I waded through mud to ask the driver if I could follow him out, using his tracks. He agreed. I didn't ask him who he was or why he had come to the camp. No one except some of the Pima people knew where we were. I followed him to the pavement, moving slowly in the track of the truck. The truck driver stopped on the pavement. I thanked him for rescuing me. I still don't know why I didn't think to ask him why he had come to our camp and how he knew its location. I was concerned only about being rescued. As I drove on I saw the truck still stopped on the pavement. Eventually I found the camp members in the facilities of a small community school. It was only after some time for reflection that I realized the utter incongruity of my rescue.

Today there is an escalating demurral of anything mystical; anything that cannot stand up to scientific explanation. Science is a marvelous tool to understand the "how" of phenomena but it does not answer the "why." "Why" relates to values and meaning and has been the focus of religion and philosophy since humankind

developed consciousness. Because both are subjective, they remain suspect in the eyes of societies worshipful of science. The urge to know the "unknowable" is deep in the human spirit and has led to all the great religions and philosophies. Because the effort is human, it has also bred negative results, often creating confusion. But the human spirit is resilient in its search for unattainable "truth." If that search is honest and not just a cover for selfish motives, enlightenment results and along the way paranormal evidence can occur. In my case that evidence was dramatic, appearing over a number of years. It didn't reveal "truth," but it was empirical evidence of the reality of dimensions beyond our world and of the capacity of interaction between dimensions. Paranormal action in animals also testifies to the ubiquity of spirit in our dimension beyond that of human beings.

All of this gives breadth and depth to our cultivation of "spirit," providing a parameter that takes spirit out of the context of fantasy into elevated relevance. It feeds the deep longing in human beings to find meaning in life and gives underpinning to religious feeling and projection. It has had a major effect in my life and has given me insight into the deep spirituality of traditional Native Americans. My hope is that its articulation here may help others find deeper spirituality.

A principal concern of the Two Circles is the welfare of Indian Youth. Indian young people have faced overwhelming odds extending back to state imposition of boarding schools in the 1870s. The Two Circles youth programs and activities build cultural awareness and pride

which are the antithesis of the boarding school experience that did so much damage to Indian children deep into the 20th century. The system was created by an army officer, Colonel Richard H. Pratt, who modeled the schools after a prison school he developed for Indian prisoners of war. He is reported to have said, "All the Indian there is in the race should be dead. Kill the Indian and save the man." His principle permeated the boarding school system, the goal of which was not quality education but eradication, through regimentation and abuse, of all cultural and spiritual qualities that define Indians. It was a tool for cultural genocide. One of the Traditional Circle leaders, José Lucero, Santa Clara Pueblo, said this about Indian boarding schools:

"Under the guise of educating Indian children, those from the ages of six years and older were taken from their homes, families, and natural world homelands, some forcefully, and enrolled in schools which were actually internment camps set up by the U.S. government and various churches to be assimilated and stripped of all contact in being who they were. They were abused emotionally, physically, sexually, and spiritually.

"The instructors/teachers created havoc among these young people. It was a paradise for pedophiles. There was total disrespect for innocent children.

"Today there is much interest and concern regarding child abuse and minor infractions which can be compared to much greater atrocities experienced by Indian children.

"Upon returning to their homes, many who survived this so-called "educational process" were ashamed, quiet and withdrawn. Some continued to carry on the abuse practices they had encountered and learned at these schools within their families and communities. Others turned to

alcohol or committed suicide, not wanting to live. Only the spiritually strong survived and were able to forgive their abusers but they never forgot what happened to them."

Tens of thousands of Indian children have suffered the abuse of boarding schools, with repercussion still resonating in Indian communities. Contemporary adults who experienced boarding schools testify to its shocking levels of abuse. Being deprived of parental love and guidance from age six to young adult years created dysfunctional individuals, many of whom carried the abuses they suffered into their own communities. Along with other elements of repression, the boarding school experience placed a heavy burden on the Native American community. The Two Circles' youth programs, led by traditional Elders, are designed to reclaim the traditional heritage in the lives of young people, building strong cultural and spiritual identity and more stable communities.

Along with Elders and Youth councils, youth programs were designed and implemented in many communities. One of the most dramatic was held in the Pima community south of Phoenix. The gang mentality originating in inner city Phoenix had reached Pima youth. They came to an orientation meeting in gang jackets and with heads down, headphones blasting, obviously disinterested, acting disdainful. They wanted to be considered Hispanic rather than Indian because Hispanics had more status in the gang world. Two men and two women from the Elders Circle were there to work with them. In addition to scheduled programs, they were told that two Elders would remain by a fire close by and would talk with anyone who came to them. The first day only one or two came to the fire. By the end of four days, the whole group was there often and

no one wanted to leave. The spirit of their heritage encoded in their makeup, and lying just under the surface, had been released, giving them the integrity of identity and a new awareness and pride in being Indian. This process occurs each time youth have the opportunity to spend time with Traditional Elders.

A new program was called for by the Elders after a Circle gathering at the Sapa Dawn Center in Yelm, Washington, near Puget Sound where a group of Nisqually women brought a story of a dysfunctional community in which those in authority were part of the problem. They did not expect help but wanted to unburden themselves to a sympathetic audience. The upshot was the Two Circles development of a family program called "Healing the Future," designed to reach families with reinforcement of traditional values and skills giving them the mental, emotional, and spiritual tools of their heritage as a means of countering the encroachment of drugs, alcohol, apathy, and outside inter-ference into both families and communities. It was adjunct to existing youth programs.

Meanwhile the communications objectives were being served. Speakers from the Elders Circle singly and in groups were scheduled in venues across the country, particularly in universities, town halls, and church organizations. They appeared in national convenings including an unusual occurrence at the October 1993 Parliament of the World's Religions in Chicago. Ninety-year-old Tom Yellowtail, a Crow from the Elders Circle, gave the opening prayer. More than 5,000 spokespeople representing religions from around the world were there to talk about how religious tradition could impact world problems. At one point, contention among delegates became heated to a point of disruption. Tom took the stage and calmed the group with

the sense of authority and quiet assurance of traditional Native Americans.

In order to protect its grass roots integrity, the Two Circles did not indulge in promotion or advertising but word-of-mouth raised its image both domestically and abroad. The American Indian Institute became a source of information for people wanting access to the Traditional Circle.

The growing reputation of the Traditional Circle as advocates for conservation and protection of Earth's resources came to the attention of world leaders concerned with environmental issues. In 1987 we received an invitation for Elders Circle participation in the Fourth World Wilderness Congress convened in Denver and Estes Park, Colorado, in which 1,600 delegates from 64 countries considered conservation of the earth. Fourteen members of the Elders Circle participated in the event. Oren Lyons, Onondaga, representing the Circle, was a keynote speaker, along with 87-year-old Magqubu Ntombela, a Zulu of the old tradition from South Africa. Magqubu created an exotic appearance, dressed in a traditional Zulu garment of lion skin, leopard skin tribal headband, and narrow bandoliers of beadwork.

A highlight of the Congress was the appearance of Magqubu with Oren Lyons, together on stage expressing concern for the health and capacity of the natural world to sustain life. They were visual, as well as oral, proof of the power and eloquence of indigenous people functionally relevant to today's world. The fact that indigenous speakers from cultures a world apart held perspectives and values

in common, and in sharp contrast with much of the industrialized world, meant that the voice of uncounted millions of indigenous people were present in the Congress.

This may have been the first time that representatives of indigenous peoples of Africa and North America appeared together on a world stage. That natives from different continents, origins, and lifeways spoke with a common voice had a profound effect.

In our follow-up meeting upon the conclusion of the Congress, Vance Martin, President of the WILD Foundation which has connections in South Africa, said, "The combination of the Traditional Circle of Elders along with Magqubu Natombela had a great impact on the Congress. We should invite representatives of both the Elders Circle and the American Indian Institute to come to South Africa." We talked about it at length. Vance met with the South African Ambassador and other officials in Washington, D.C., and arranged meetings for us. The idea of inviting the creators of a new approach to racial understanding and cooperation among cultures to speak in South Africa was well received. We met with officials of both South Africa and the United States. On a little island in the Potomac River, an oasis of the natural world in the congestion of Washington, D.C., we made final arrangements for Oren Lyons and me, representing the Two Circles, to visit South Africa. We had several objectives: to make the first official contact between Native Americans and Zulus, the largest native group in Natal Province; to experience a foot safari with the Wilderness Leadership School in Natal for possible replication in Montana with Indian guides; to speak at University symposia in Durban, Natal Province; and for additional meetings which Vance Martin would arrange.

The Wilderness Leadership School foot safari program has an outstanding record of bringing movers and shakers from around the world to a wilderness experience with Zulu guides. During the safari, visitors are away from telephones and all outside distractions, giving them time to absorb the peace and meaning of wilderness. They are able to experience the skills and values of Zulus in their environment, as well as hear them talk about those values in their lives and in the long history of their people; values that impinge upon human relationships, conservation, and constructive relationships with the natural world, and provide a new look at the impact of human beings on the earth. All these issues are crucial in today's world. The Wilderness Leadership School has achieved remarkable results.

Our foot safari in the Umfalozi wilderness was led by 88-year-old Magqubu Ntombela, our friend from the Wilderness Congress in Denver. Without the protection of Land Rovers, natural forces have the upper hand and human life becomes part of the food chain.

We were first given a paper to sign that said in effect "you might die but we cannot be held responsible." Comforting. Magqubu was the only one who carried a rifle. We proceeded in single file with six feet between each person so that a lion or other animal in a hurry could get through.

Our first camp was on a rhino trail above the Umfalozi River. Magqubu took a bucket to get water. I followed him because at his age I thought he might need help bringing the water to camp. Ignoring me, he put the full bucket on his *head* and walked up to camp without a drop spilled. I saw Magqubu with new eyes. We did not have tents, but kept a fire all night for protection. Each of us was given a watch to keep the fire going; mine was from midnight to

2:00 AM. The African night is mysterious. It is a time when animals feed, and while their activities cannot be seen, they can be heard. Sometimes the night would be filled with cries and sounds both baffling and alarming. There would be sounds of brush crashing followed by a loud thud, then silence. High-pitched screams punctuated the dark. Fire-keepers had a flashlight. When pointed into the bush around camp, eyes would be reflected; sometimes the eyes were six inches apart, the animal both unknown and silent. The fire protected us. During the trip, Magqubu maneuvered to get us close to Africa's large animals, though always with safety in mind. At rest periods he talked about his life in the bush. He spoke with respect and a feeling of relationship with the animals that had been as much a part of his life as people. He spoke of the bush which had met his people's needs and given them life they hoped to pass on to the next generation.

He spoke in Zulu with interpretation by the late Ian Player, founder of the Wilderness Leadership School. Magqubu and Ian Player could not have had a closer relationship; but while Macqubu was one of us during the day, he did not eat with us or bathe with us in the river. He slept in a tent some distance away from us.

Apartheid had its iron grip even in the wilderness. Macqubu changed what would have been an interesting trip through an exotic environment into a life-enhancing experience.

We were excited about using the Wilderness Leadership School model in the Montana wilderness with Indians as guides. It would give participants not only an experience in the value and understanding of wilderness, but also respect for Native people in whose care they were entrusted, and who fit the wilderness environment. It would be a lesson in two critical conservation efforts: the preservation of the world's remaining wilderness along with preservation of the heritage of indigenous people whose lives are guided by values learned in living close to the natural world. Unfortunately, the scope of our Two Circles affairs did not allow us to develop the program here, though it remains high among our priorities.

There were experiences in the African wilderness that could not be duplicated in Montana's wilderness. Natal Parks Department officials took us on a horseback trip to Lesotho, a small country in the highest part of the surrounding South Africa, some of which is above timberline. I was horseback again but missed our Western saddles. They used McLellan saddles, created for the U.S. Cavalry by someone who had a grudge against Cavalrymen. It was an all-day ride and into the night, in the rain.

As we approached our destination in the quiet darkness of a trail through thick timber we heard the most beautiful singing: pure, liquid women's voices in two parts that could have come from trained voices in one of our cities. The idea of being in one of the most remote spots in Africa, in darkness, and hearing—from nowhere—music beautifully sung, touched my musician's heart so deeply that I still remember its shock and impact. That an element of one of humanity's greatest arts could occur here in absolute isolation testified to the universal power of music and touched my spirit with its overwhelming beauty. Later I learned that it came from a chapel back in the bush.

We were guests of an American agricultural experiment station. A small native community of round, thatched-roofed stone huts was a short distance away. Chip Kamber, a female Wilderness Leadership School staff member, and I decided to visit the village. A mistake, since our party was involved in activities at the station and no one knew about our leaving. As we approached the village we saw a white flag on one of the huts. We met a lady with a baby in a carrier on her back, a universal alliance among women. Chip and the lady talked excitedly about the baby, neither understanding the other. By gesture the lady invited us to come with her to the hut with the flag, the color indicating the quality and state of beer being made. The area was jammed with people.

The door of the hut was a low, oblong opening, without cover. Chip ducked in with no trouble. When I tried, a hand hit my chest with a sharp blow. I backed out while the elder who belonged to the hand emerged, talking in a high and excited pitch. Noticing a teenage boy with clothes differing from the rest and finding he spoke some English, I asked what the harangue was about. In halting words he said, "He-wants-you-to-shoot-him," pointing to my camera. I had no film left but since I was at a distinct disadvantage and in a delicate position, I said, "Sure, tell him I'll take his picture."

His wife arrived, wrapped in a small blue blanket around her traditional dress. They posed proudly and I snapped the camera, returning to the hut and entering with no trouble. Musicians were playing handmade instruments and people were attempting to dance, but it was so crowded they could only stay in one spot in a kind of jig. There were no windows; the only light came from a fire in the center.

Looking for a place to sit, I noticed an open spot across from the fire. As I was sitting down, a hand grabbed my arm pulling me away. In the dim light I had not noticed it was the women's side. I was escorted out; this time I got the message. Chip emerged saying, "I think we should get out of here—now." The men inside had become too attentive to the only non-native, blonde woman. We were getting ominous stares as we emerged from the hut. We slipped out but had gone only a short way when every child at the celebration, from those who could walk to teenagers, came running after us: 30 or 40. Language was no help so we continued walking. Having this group follow us to camp would not make the Centre happy.

Chip had an idea. "Let's take their picture. It worked for you," she said. So by gesture and pointing to my camera, she got across the idea that we would take their picture. They were all smiles, the young ones running back to get the babies. They lined up making sure the babies could be seen. I took their picture, again with no film in the camera. Everyone talked excitedly to each other and to us in their language, and we responded in ours. As we left they went slowly back to the celebration.

Chip and I were very foolish in going to the village alone and entering a celebration fueled by beer. No one in our group knew where we were and if circumstances had become difficult we would have had no help; only later did we learn of the potential dangers of our presence alone at the celebration. That said, our experience was memorable and intense in ways closed to most outsiders. But we would not repeat it.

Our presence in Africa was not to advocate a political position, but rather to find common human ground that would provide a basis for living well on our planet with minimum human conflict and destruction of the environment. We did express our perspectives to those who asked

for it. We participated in symposia at Pietermaritzburg University, spoke at a University in Durban, and had meetings at the Institute of International Affairs in Johannesburg, hosted by the Department of Foreign Affairs.

The most chilling meeting was a lunch with the South African Secretary of State. Our answer to his question regarding our opinion following our on-the-ground experience was, "We believe there is still a window of opportunity to involve all people in the processes of government without bloodshed, but it is closing rapidly."

"You may be right, but if it happens it will last one day," he said.

We met with Mangosuthu Buthelezi, Chief Minister of KwaZulu, and his cabinet at Ulundi, capital of KwaZulu-Natal Province, situated deep in the bush; at the time it was a quaint combination of ancient culture with modern elements. We stayed in a Holiday Inn, its rooms low and built around a courtyard filled with grazing zebras. The two-story capitol was like none other, being covered with inch-square blue tile, the interior finished with the best African wood. Buthelezi was a courtly figure who spoke perfect Oxford English.

Oren Lyons brought a message of peace and empathy for the Zulu people. He spoke of family connection among indigenous peoples of the world and of values they hold in common. The unity of spirit in the room was exciting for me; I was used to it in Native American circles, but I was impressed to find it among people half a world away. In thanking Oren, Buthelezi called the talk "pearls of wisdom." Our meeting concluded with an exchange of gifts.

There were two deep impressions from our visit to South Africa. One was the unique "feel" of the country; the air had special buoyancy and the Outback, with its profusion of plant and animal life beyond any other place, had a feeling of antiquity as if one were going back in time, or to another planet. The second impression related to city life: it was almost a police state. In spite of rhetoric to the contrary, there was an undercurrent of feeling, an uneasiness resulting from the fear that the tensions of Apartheid were approaching a crisis point. It was apparent in discussions at University Symposia, in the guarded way government officials spoke to us, and in conversations with civic leaders. Yet the circumstances of daily life gave no indication of cracks in the grip of Apartheid. We also sensed a concern on the part of responsible people regarding the image of South Africa in the outside world. It was not surprising to us that the crisis arrived a couple years later, but we were deeply surprised and gratified that Nelson Mandala became President of South Africa in a peaceful process, and that Apartheid was dismantled without bloodshed. All the evidence we had seen said that it would not happen that way.

One of the great failings of human beings is a tendency to categorize the worth and status of others within the context of race and ethnicity. I never felt its depth until working with Native Americans, and was not prepared for the vitriol in mainstream society. Since I was a member of that society, working with traditional Native people and soliciting support for them by speaking to many groups, I became a target for pent-up emotions; most were negative, some were positive, but all were condescending.

People—white people—would say things to me they would not to others. I was surprised by the degree of hate they expressed. Some of it was directed at me because I was the "Indians' advocate," and some was directed at Indians. In a question and answer period following a talk in a small town in western Montana, a middle-aged lady was red-faced as she listed all the negative things about Native Americans that she and others had experienced. She was incensed. My responses only brought new invectives. At other times, the hate would be cushioned in the toned-down rhetoric of education; in a sense, that was even worse because it was insidious rather than blatant.

Steve Browning, longtime Institute Board Chair, was one of the few non-Indians who could articulate the situation we found ourselves in. He was co-founder of a successful Helena, Montana law firm. He also served on the staff of former U.S. Senator and ambassador to China, Max Baucus; Steve was involved in civil rights issues that came before lawmakers on Capitol Hill.

Steve explained, "When I moved to Montana, I was surprised, even shocked, to hear comments by many Montanans expressing a strong prejudice against Indians. These people generally regarded Indians as shiftless, drunken, and worthless or all three. Instead of the negative stereotypes that I was accustomed to hearing back East about African Americans, I was now hearing the same thing about Native Americans. White people are completely ignorant of the profound wisdom of traditional Indian elders. While I readily admit to being ignorant of traditional Indian wisdom, Bob Staffanson sparked in me a profound reverence for nature. I wanted to learn more. Bob is a great teacher, and the Two Circles that he helped forge have been a great classroom for me and others to

help, in our own small way, insure that ancient wisdom is passed on to coming generations of elders and youth."

The kind of responses that I've encountered over the years and which persist today generally fall into these categories:

Apologists. While sympathetic to Native American conditions there is usually a lack of insight into the moral base of traditional cultures. There are traces of political correctness but understanding is often superficial.

Wannabes. Those who feel that Indians hold special insights and want to penetrate their inner circles to obtain those insights. They are takers who lack basic human protocol.

Do-gooders. People aware of the oppression of Native Americans but whose answer is to make them more like us without questioning if that fits who they are.

Romanticists. Those who consider Native Americans quaint, valuing the externals of a colorful past: dress, dances, pow wows, textile and ceramic art; believing these are the true elements of Native American cultures and holding the practitioners up as objects of veneration.

Antagonists. Replicators of hate who do not realize they are projecting their own insecurities onto a race of people.

Open and un-prejudiced minds. Fewest in number, but the only hope for a prejudice-free society. Most have an intuitive understanding that indigenous people have something we once had but lost: a spiritual relationship to all life and the comfort of fitting into an ancient system that has sustained life over time. In our society, that relationship has been sacrificed for the benefit of a rapacious economic engine.

The colorful Danish author, Isak Dinesen (the pen

name of Karen Dinesen Blixen) wrote eloquently about her relationship to Native people as proprietor of a colonial farm in Kenya. It is testimony to the positive results of mutual respect and acceptance on a basic human level:

The discovery of the dark races was to me a magnificent enlargement of all my world.

If someone had an ear for music and happened to hear music for the first time when he was already grown up; their cases might have been similar to mine.

The Natives were Africa in flesh and blood. The extinct volcano of Lonqnot, the broad Minosa trees, the Elephant and the Giraffe were not more truly Africa than the Natives were. All were expressions of one idea, variations on one theme. We ourselves, in our constant hurry, often jar with the landscape. The Natives are in accord with it and when the tan and dark-eyed people travel—always one by one, so that even the great Native veins of traffic are narrow footpaths, or work the soil or herd the cattle, or hold their big dances, or tell you a tale, it is Africa wandering, dancing and entertaining you.

Blixen interacted with African native people in Kenya from 1914 through 1931. In those years she came to hold them in high regard; but there was always an unbridgeable barrier between them based on race, class, status, and culture. She represented (an arguably) more benign and admirable attitude toward Native people, much improved over earlier generations when the slave trade was rampant; but for her, Africans remained "other." There was no sense of human equality. In our safari, that was clearly illustrated by Zulu guide Magqubu Ntombela's strict adherence to protocol. During much of the day he was one of us; but at mealtime, when we bathed in the river, and when we slept, he always remained separate. The separation of Apartheid was strong even among the best of friends. Only a short

time later Apartheid was officially dismantled; however, no state action can change the feeling of "other" among white, brown, and dark people. That has to be done individually.

The crux of our work with traditional Native Americans is to tear down the barrier that creates the notion of "other" between human beings, and help them in any way to maintain their identity and their heritage in the face of overpowering negative pressure. Blixen says the discovery of the dark races was "a magnificent enlargement of all my world." My discovery of traditional Native Americans was a magnificent enlargement of my spirit. There is a difference. From the beginning, I recognized no barrier between me and the people to whom I offered friendship and support. Our connection was on the basis of human equality, a spiritual bond in which none of the divisive elements refined over countless generations apply. With barriers down, the genius of both societies can flow unimpeded in both directions.

I believe the Two Circles has achieved much in reducing those barriers and that all have benefitted; but it is I who has benefited most. Association with traditional Native people, whom I consider the finest associates I have had, has added a dimension missing in my spirit. We are still different people: I cannot be one of them and they cannot be one of my people. We have different genes, different heritage, different life journeys; but we respect those differences in each other and move beyond them to what we have in common: humanity. One people. The exciting thing about that is liberation: liberation from the negatives that hold us back from connection to all people as equals, with freedom to be who we are and to connect as human beings in building lives that rise above conflict

and discord to create one human family; to realize the best that is in all of us.

Unlike Karen Dinesen Blixen, my discovery of the native people of North America was not a sudden epiphany but a lifelong process. For her, coming to know the native people of Kenya was abrupt, resulting in an interesting and captivating new perspective on humanity; but she remained the same person. For me, association with traditional Native Americans on a deeper level changed my life. I have a bond with them that goes beyond blood to spirit. I see them as family: cousins who represent another side of the family, completing the word for me.

My spiritual journey had its first apex in the rarified atmosphere of great classical music, spilling over into other aspects of life, top down. Native Americans brought a new, inclusive perspective, bottom up. In music I was in a hurry, consumed by the demands of an exacting profession, striving always for a higher reach. Traditional Native Americans calmed my spirit, letting elements of inclusiveness, which were always there, blossom into the prominence they deserve, achieving balance of spirit. Undergirding this relationship is a shared belief in powers beyond us, called by many different names, which have shaping capacities for us and which need our recognition and cultivation to achieve our true destiny as human beings.

When structuring the Two Circles, I was still operating in the context of mainstream society's terms. Oren Lyons often tells a story about our earliest meetings. He explains that I told him that I had funding for three years and by that time we would be well organized and independent. It

took a full five years just to build enough trust so that we could successfully work together. By the end of thirteen years, the Traditional Circle of Indian Elders and Youth had gained enough respect to be invited to major events around the world.

In 1990 we were invited to participate in the *Global Forum of Spiritual and Parliamentary Leaders* in Moscow, Soviet Union. The forum brought worldwide political and faith leaders together to discuss and influence each other in dealing with human survival in an age of potentially catastrophic environmental problems, growing interdependence of nations, and the need for more harmonious and compassionate existence among all people. We brought delegates from North and South America, Africa, Hawaii, and Siberia, and Samis from the Arctic Circle.

We arrived in Moscow on a cold January day. Satisfying customs at the airport was a problem for some of our delegation. The Hopis and Iroquois were traveling on their own passports. The Hopi passports confirmed validation "as long as the grass grows and the water flows." Typically, the Russians found this difficult to understand. Some of them laughed with backs turned. The Hopi were detained.

A very large Russian came to me with my passport saying, "**Problem**," in a deep-voiced Russian accent. He indicated that I wait; I think they considered me subversive. The Hopi situation was resolved and I saw all my people moving through customs entry while I was still stuck, my anxiety growing. I don't know how or why but finally the large man returned with a "**No Problem**" message, and I caught up with our delegation.

We had arrived on the Russian New Year. Russians love to sing. At the hotel the room next to mine was occupied by a number of men who were singing loudly to

celebrate the New Year, and were probably lubricated with vodka. I assumed they would either become tired or run out of songs; neither happened. They didn't finish until morning and I hadn't slept. Meals were served in a hotel cafeteria where attendants offered black market caviar and other Russian delicacies; anything to get American money. There was very little meat; water was bottled.

Our delegation always began the day with a sunrise ceremony involving prayers and burning tobacco. Since there was no outside spot available, Leon Shenandoah lit a fire in a standing ash tray and conducted the ceremony.

Our first meeting was with the complete Indigenous delegation. I was struck, as I have been many times since, with the degree to which they were "family"; people who lived continents apart. The problems each faced in their home countries differed only in detail; all centered in pressures from the larger society regarding indigenous land, cultures, lifeways, language, and spirituality. The discussion was not about what their message should be, but about the best ways to deliver the message they held in common. The impact of the Indigenous delegation was deep, and I hoped was destined to make a difference.

There were a thousand delegates from 60 countries, including world print news organizations and global television provided by two satellite networks. Most striking was the appointment of Audrey Shenandoah, a Clan Mother from Onondaga and a member of the Traditional Circle, as one of two keynote speakers, and the other was Gro Harlem Brundtland, former Prime Minister of Norway: two females, one a recognized world leader, the other bringing the Indigenous voice to a world audience, perhaps for the first time, by a female representative.

It was a good beginning. Audrey Shenandoah's remarks

concerned the state of the earth and the physical and spiritual environment of the human race. It resonated with ancient wisdom, introducing the audience to the spirituality of Native Americans, an outlook in which gratitude and respect trump greed and avarice. Audrey's message and later ones by indigenous delegates were the same as those I had heard many years ago, messages that changed my life. Now those messages were being heard by movers and shakers around the world and, through television, to countless people.

I don't know if lives were changed, but I do believe that sensitive people could not have listened to the ancient wisdom of people living close to the earth without having been deeply moved. That message would not be presented in that way by any other people.

The colorful dress of some of the Indigenous delegation drew media attention. The Haidas from British Columbia were spectacular in their bird headdresses. At intervals within and between sessions people crowded around Oren Lyons, Leon Shenandoah, Thomas Bayacya, and others to talk personally with them and listen. A delegate from equatorial Africa was conspicuous in wearing a heavy down coat at all times, both indoors and outside. It was his first experience with cold weather. If his room was like mine he probably slept in it.

The Indigenous delegation prepared a statement entitled *We Are the Peoples of the Earth*, maintaining that indigenous cultures have provided the only historical models of sustainable development and outlining the qualities needed for a sustainable future. In part it said, "Earth suffers ill treatment because of lack of respect ... We must relearn the lessons of tolerance, generosity, and love that will bring peace and a future for our children ... The path

to human survival means that we embrace a new age characterized by a global cultural pluralism which celebrates all races, ethnicities, and religions of humankind … Indigenous cultures can help provide inspiration for a future in which love is extended beyond the confines of human society to embrace the natural world … Earth is our place: let us believe in it and take care of it as we take care of children, our parents, and grandparents."

A film crew from Japan arranged interviews with several of our Elders Circle members. As soon as the recording equipment was erected in Red Square, Russian people in fur hats congregated around the Elders, mothers holding children up to see them. The Elders spoke to the crowd, the warmth of their message shining through a language barrier. Native Americans are among the best ambassadors for the United States. Thomas Banyacya invited everyone to visit him at his home in Hopi.

The closing event was held in the Kremlin's impressive St. George's Hall. Mikhail Gorbachev closed the forum with his impressions of its accomplishment and its suggested actions for all to take. The spiritual closing was made by Swami Paramananda, senior monk of the 12,000-year-old Shankaracharya order in India. He voiced three-thousand-year-old Vedic chants, prayers of people to all life and all the elements. Tarzie Vittachi, Celanese, said, "Who would possibly miss such a marvelously ironic, marvelously ecstatic moment, when, for the first time since 1917, a religious utterance was heard in the Kremlin—not a sotto vocé pleading for protection, but a superb human affirmation of awareness of the oneness of the human spirit."

My own overpowering response was gratification that the indigenous voice was given prominence in keynote

speeches, group reports, and plenary discussions. I am confident that ancient voices of wisdom had a positive effect on most delegates and was a catalyst for reconsidering stereotypical thinking on the part of all.

Three years before our Russian trip, a friend at the Nippon Club in New York City prevailed upon us to present an Indian art exhibition at the Club. We exhibited Indian art, sculpture, textiles, jewelry, and baskets from major private collections in the area. It was well received and resulted in an invitation from the Yomiuri Shimbun, Japan's largest newspaper, to visit Japan for a week to plan an Indian cultural presentation there in 1988. Fred Dockstader, Oneida, and I flew to Tokyo. Following exchange of greetings at Yomiuri Shimbun headquarters, the first question asked of me was, "Do you live in a big house?" That surprised me until I realized that restricted space in Japan's urban areas makes spacious houses a luxury beyond most people.

My experience that evening in my hotel room served as an example of Japanese efficiency in utilizing space. By extending my arms I could almost touch opposing walls; but unlike my Russian hotel room, it had everything I needed including a comfortable bed and quiet neighbors.

There is a mystique about American Indians in Japan which runs deep, probably stemming from ancient feelings of connection. There is a report of finding a DNA pattern in the remains of a seven-thousand-year-old man in the swamps of Florida similar to that of modern-day Japanese. In subsequent events in Japan I have been struck by the physical similarities of West Coast Indians and the Japanese.

Through Yomiuri Shimbun auspices we arranged to bring Indian dancers to Tokyo for ceremonies, launching

the American Train in Japan: a program in which multiple rail cars, each containing materials about an American Company, would travel Japan for a year, stopping for exhibition at each community on the railway. It would be launched in Tokyo with a week of American cultural events during which Indian dancers would perform. We also planned an exhibition of American Indian art and artifacts in project facilities.

Restaurant meals in Tokyo tend to be minimal and lacking in meat compared to those in our country. A friend took me to an "American" restaurant, which served food in the quantity and quality of American cuisine. Its specialty was steak, the only place in Tokyo I saw steak served. It also had an American atmosphere. Several Japanese men in cowboy hats, boots, and chaps played guitars and sang American country-western music, a sight that stays in my mind to this day.

All areas of Indian country were involved in the American Indian Dance Theater group performing in an outdoor arena. The dancers could not have had a more appreciative audience. Crowds gathered to get a glimpse of them. Between sets, mothers brought their children up close to see them and to talk with them, even through a language barrier. The dancers were engulfed by people wanting to connect with them in some way. The dancers' demeanor and courtesy in meeting with Japanese people could not have been better. I was gratified to be a part of that cross-cultural exchange. It seemed to me to be yet another verification of the need identified at the headwaters gathering, ten years earlier.

During times when the dancers were not performing, we explored Tokyo, which for several of us included a visit with Mike Mansfield, fellow Montanan and American

Ambassador to Japan. I remember the walls of the hall leading to the Ambassador's office being covered with Winold Reiss 1920s paintings of Blackfoot Indians. I don't know the feelings of my Indian friends, but I was struck with the stereotype of Indians being stuck in their colorful past as if that were the end of their relevance.

Enthusiasm for the Indian dancers and our week-long interaction with the people of Japan were a revelation of how respect for common humanity and appreciation of individual gifts and strengths can create mutually positive responses and bring out the best in human beings. The fact that the Indians were treated like celebrities by some was not the central issue. The profound result was that Indians were given equal status as human beings and were accepted with appreciation for the gifts without prejudice. How tragic that this does not happen regularly in our country.

The American Embassy was highly supportive. Embassy official, Keith Bovetti, said: "Truly the activities of the American Indian Institute are far reaching, and, I believe, significant to our very existence. Indigenous people are the thread that runs through the world which, unknown to the majority, holds the fabric of humanity to the hem of Mother Earth. Clearly the Elders have the role of bringing the continents together, having their physical and spiritual origins on all continents: Western Hemisphere, Asia, the Pacific, Africa, and Europe."

Also in 1988 I was invited to join Secretary of Commerce, William Verity, Jr.'s group of six people traveling to Japan to promote more trade with the United States. Each person represented an industry or product; we were hoping to penetrate the Japanese trade barriers. My specialty was American Indian products, particularly

Southwest textiles and ceramics. We met with leaders of business and industry. In one memorable meeting, the CEO of Toyota Corporation told Secretary Verity about a book by an American author in which economic imperialism was being criticized. Secretary Verity's immediate response was, "You read too many books." His easy manner and lack of pretense created a comfortable environment in which the difficult issues of trade barriers could be discussed. Each of us met separately with specialists in our products. I met with heads of department store chains. There was genuine interest in the high quality work of Indian weavers, ceramicists, jewelers, and artists, and how marketing in Japan would proceed if trade conditions were favorable. I took detailed information with emphasis on dealing with Indians on their terms. Upon returning to the United States, the information gathered in Japan was given to prominent Indian marketers with suggestions of how it might best be pursued, as our organization could not integrate a major marketing program.

Two years after the Russia trip, in 1992, the passing of five hundred years since the arrival of Columbus was noted widely in the United States, gaining considerable media coverage. Notably absent was the perspective of Native Americans. Together with the Threshold Foundation, we planned and implemented a program in which delegations from the Traditional Circle of Indian Elders appeared in venues across the country giving their perspective of the event and its consequences for the people who had lived here for centuries.

Those consequences decimated the indigenous pop-

ulation, along with their cultures and value systems. The only wisdom indigenous to this hemisphere was crushed, its people driven into small enclaves with their spiritual and moral heritage forced to go underground. The loss of a spiritual compass pushed many into the limbo between cultures, bringing the scourge of alcohol. Members of the Traditional Circle are leaders in a group throughout North America who survived intact and in whom the future of the indigenous heritage is held.

Statements from members of the Traditional Circle were given to media outlets and appearances across the country were scheduled for Circle members. At the invitation of Reuben Snake, Winnebago, a memorable appearance occurred at Winnebago in eastern Nebraska. Circle leaders were present.

NBC sent a crew from Omaha to cover the event. Each of the delegates spoke eloquently about the consequences of five centuries of oppression of their people and of the survival of a heritage that remains against all odds. Typical of traditional speakers, there was no rancor in their delivery, but a clear statement of facts of which most people are unaware or have swept under the rug of conscience.

Their message was one of optimism that the divisiveness separating races and ethnicities will ultimately be resolved. They believe that the Native people in whom the traditional heritage runs deep are positioned well to advance that process. They have been subject to intense oppression and have emerged without malice and are committed to using the wisdom and experience of countless generations to promote peace, harmony, and respect among all people. They are committed to ending mindless destruction of the natural world and all elements that support

life. That is the mission of the Two Circles and the hope of the world.

For more than 40 years, the Two Circles have had a major influence within indigenous societies of North America and across cultures around the world. The evidence is recorded in these pages, but the example of its structure can also be an important legacy. To our knowledge, there is no comparable enterprise involving major elements of society with a long history of conflict and antagonism that have come together to reconcile under terms similar to that of the Two Circles. Normal reconciliation is through politics, in which there are winners and losers or a stalemate leaving the root causes intact. The Two Circles avoided politics; its founders represent spiritual rather than political positions, with the word "spiritual" used in its broad sense.

When ground rules were established there was no fanfare, no publicity raising expectations, or opposition from people who knew nothing of the process. There was no press release or pictures. The roots grew slowly, discreetly, and were tested by action and time. Within that process, success was first manifested at grass roots level and carried by word of mouth. Even so, there was considerable opposition in both societies. The status quo in the non-Indian world was threatened by the new coalition, as was newly awakened militancy in the Indian world. Because we were essentially underground to avoid curiosity seekers and opponents as much as possible in both societies, the opposition could be contained; however, because "moccasin telegraph" is effective and any new enterprise inevitably creates waves, zealots on both sides tried their

best to stop us. In order to avoid the racism label, non-Indians would use competition for funding as an excuse. Or they maintained that our goal was to keep Indians mired in the past, and that economic help, not reinforcing "superstition" would bring them into the 20th century. The real reason, though, for opposition was racism, the depth of which surprised me. I lost many friends. Racism also influenced the Indian side: what business did I, a white man, have intruding into their internal affairs, and anyway those "old guys" represented the past; the new militants could take care of things without interference.

As success and growth continued, positive responses became deeper in both societies until opposition played out. A new and effective cross-cultural change engine had been achieved from bottom up rather than top down, its roots secure and its potential unlimited. That potential has been realized in considerable measure; with wise guidance, its future both domestically and worldwide is bright. The key will be the next couple of generations. The wise ones at the first meeting of the Two Circles in 1977 said, "An evaluation of what we are proposing cannot be made until it has passed through more generations." That is to say, it must resonate beyond our time and be carried by people of vision to reach its potential. Many of those Elders are now gone. Our task is to deliver it to the next generation with vision and impact intact and growing. We won't see the Promised Land, but we began the march.

If we remove layers of ego, self-interest, prejudice, greed, hate, and the will to dominate, we find that human beings everywhere have the same fundamental needs and aspirations. The essential aspects of each of us are in all others, and the differences are minor compared to the commonalities. If we could just understand this premise,

all the barriers that separate us would fall. Conflict would not disappear but it would be manageable within humane parameters. The obscenity of physical conflict would be an anomaly, not a dominating reality in our world.

Traditional Native Americans represent that state of mind more than any group I know. Having been recipients of unspeakable treatment over uncounted generations, most have emerged with spirit intact; without hate, and with understanding of the human connection among all people and with all life and the elements that support life. This spirit, the essence of which can be reduced to love without sentimental overtones, is infectious. I felt it first many years ago among the Blood Indians of Canada and it has been reinforced over all the time I have worked with them. They have made me a better person and I am privileged to be an advocate for them. We must not quit trying. The contemporary world is consumed by escalating conflicts. Violence is the common solution, which may create a pause in a dispute, but only deepens its root causes. Eventually, the lack of solution creates the seemingly impenetrable barriers seen in so many current examples.

If people of open minds and compassionate spirits on both sides could come together, and recognize that shared humanity and spirit outweigh any differences or any concept of "other," conflict resolution could then happen without winners and losers; with hostility softened if not destroyed. When that happens it becomes contagious. The Two Circles are proof that it is possible.

POSTLUDE

Witness to Spirit

Spirit is the thread that connects and makes sense of the radical life-work contrasts outlined in this book. Spirit is a common concept without precise connotation, because it can't be captured and measured. Science denies its reality for that reason; but even so, most people have a feeling for it if not a precise definition. Spirit is a force which lifts us into a realm beyond ego-driven needs and allows our highest aspirations to grow and integrate. Spirit provides a cosmic recognition of the sanctity of humanity and the natural world, as well as awareness of forces beyond our understanding that are responsible for, and impact, both. Too often tied exclusively to dogma, spirit is the force that allows us to live full and complete lives.

It is the one element in our makeup that many people, including some neuroscientists, believe is indestructible. They agree that it is activated through the brain but hold that it does not originate there, any more than music originates in a radio; and that its source in another dimension means it will return there when the body which houses it dies. It has many names: spirit, soul, consciousness, animating life principle. Regardless of name, anyone who experiences it in depth knows its reality. Human beings tend to give the bulk of their attention to life's short-term needs while neglecting the cultivation of spirit, which carries keys to the ultimate meaning and glory of life. Spirit in human beings can grow over time or it can atrophy. We have strict guidelines for maintaining physical health but neglect spiritual health. All body processes decline with age; spirit is the only element that, if nurtured, sees only growth. It is the greatest challenge of life. Spirit needs no special set of circumstances to grow, as has been evidenced by the accomplishments of spiritual leaders throughout history who have prevailed against the most egregious conditions.

My spiritual journey began in isolation, with the natural world as teacher. I grew up on horseback in the outback of Montana. A good horse gives a young boy a feeling of invincibility, but the natural world intervenes with a tempering influence. Riding alone in high country my horse provided both security and capacity. I was dependent upon him, and was actually the weakest of the community of life encountered there. The abundant wildlife, as well as domestic animals, fit within the environment and could take care of themselves. I was an intruder: dependent on other life. Dependency is the mother of humility, which is central to spirit. Dependency also creates an appreciation of community, another ingredient of spirit. I learned to view elements of the natural world not as utilitarian objects, but as parts of an integrated system; each having a function and purpose without which the system could not be sustained, creating a spiritual connection that affects how one feels and acts with regard to the vulnerability of the natural world and our capacity for abuse and destruction. It grounded me, providing a solid

base for spiritual growth along with a need to return periodically for spiritual refreshment. I have the same strong homing instinct for the natural world of Montana as did our horse, "Diamond," who swam the Yellowstone River every spring to return to the place where he was foaled.

My deepest spiritual growth took place in music. Called the "universal language," it is open to everyone, with impact on sentient levels from physical and emotional to the highest spiritual insights, the latter coming from music considered supreme by generations of people. Because music is the most abstract of the arts and not tied to any temporal realities, it is also the most "spiritual," taking its listeners into the spiritual stratosphere as far as their capacities will allow. To achieve greatness in the spiritual sense, music must stand the test of time confirmed by, and often enhanced by, many generations. A few composers remain at the top of that genre: Bach, Mozart, Beethoven, Brahms, among others. They're the giants; but in every generation there are a few who capture the spirit of their time in overpowering ways. If that spirit remains relevant to ongoing generations, it becomes part of a lasting legacy.

Mozart may have had the "purest" genius, and is to music what Michelangelo is to art or Shakespeare to literature. Mozart wrote music as if taking dictation, with no "Sturm und Drang" as in Beethoven. I have special affinity for the music of Beethoven. He struggled to achieve some of the most powerful music ever, and in that struggle represented the capacity of human beings to overcome limitations to reach the loftiest spiritual heights. His internal struggles were compounded by becoming totally deaf, after which he did his greatest work. I empathize with that challenge.

Each great composer represents a unique spiritual insight. Taken together, they provide windows into spirit. Advanced spiritual insights do not appear automatically, but are only achieved through time, effort, and commitment, in addition to an inherent aptitude. A fine conductor once told me he didn't feel totally equipped to do justice to a Mozart symphony until he was about 60.

During my conducting career, great music integrated forces that were nascent within me. Always sympathetic to people marginalized by society, I gained new perspective on the integrity and humanity common to all people. The pettiness and malignancy of divisiveness that separates human beings and creates debilitating categories is made clear in the process of performing great music. Standing before more than 200 musicians, people of varying age, gender, race, ethnicity, and culture in bringing to life one of the great choral/orchestral masterworks is a lesson in the unity of the human family and in love. Spirit, at its core, is love. When spirit is amplified by performing musicians, and reinforced by a sensitive audience, it creates an experience like none other. Over time it becomes a force impacting all of life. It is so deep in some musicians, particularly those who are most accomplished, that it becomes a cocoon; it dominates all elements of life: economic, social, recreational, and spiritual. While liberating in some ways, the depth of that focus can be limiting. It's like living in another world wherein you interact only with people of like mind. During my conducting tenure, it dominated my life in all the ways noted above; but it didn't have an exclusive hold: I was never a slave to music. I took breaks from the world of conducting, which enhanced other spiritual perspectives; I believe these times of renewal added new impetus to music. That balance was one of the

factors that allowed me to leave a conducting career when internal forces could no longer be denied, a decision that was incomprehensible to musicians at my level; to them, it was abandoning life. They could not imagine leaving a hard-won position held only by a favored few, running out on gifts not extravagantly given and being a traitor to a great art. But to me the decision expanded life: allowing me to reach for new goals that would broaden and enhance life. I didn't believe I was abandoning gifts so much as perfecting others that were equally, if not even more urgently, needed. I left with a clear conscience. The departure from music took a physical toll and its absence leaves an empty spot in my psyche, but its residue will continue to be sustaining. Spiritually the move was positive, contributing to broader horizons. I owe much to music and will always hold it deeply in my heart.

In entering the world of traditional Native Americans, I was as much a neophyte as I was when entering the world of music. The difference was a strong spiritual base that had been conditioned by music, providing a fertile field for growth. It was a new learning experience. The traditional Native American worldview has a spiritual base, rather than a material base, which drew me inexorably to it. There were glimpses of it early in my life, and then baptism in a Blood Indian medicine camp got my attention like being doused in cold water; it took years of learning from traditional leaders to integrate it into my being. I am my own person with my own heritage, but traditional Native Americans have fulfilled my spirit. They brought depth to the concept of "oneness" in the human family and its relationship to all life. They brought urgency to the need for respect and nurture of our little spaceship Earth that has no escape hatch. Today I have a feeling of

"oneness" with them that is deeper than blood. I am much in their debt.

Spirit has been the silver bullet in my life journey. I have cultivated it; although its consequences have the imprint of forces beyond my control. I believe spirit connects each of us to a dimension from which we came and to which we return, and that through this connection we have access to both moral and tangible influence. We all hold the capacity to cultivate spirit, to connect with our true source; but the demands of physical existence, the ego-driven needs for material accomplishment and comfort as a measure of "success," the insistence of science that our higher aspirations, including love, are simply a chemical reaction in the brain, and the drum beat of commerce telling us that materialism is the highest goal, pushes spirit into the background or entirely off our radar screen.

Love is central in spirit; not the kind of love symbolized by Cupid with a bow and arrow, but the love that is an overpowering sense of connection on levels above the functional and pragmatic. It is a confirmation of the miracle of life, which unites human beings into one family and makes all other life forms our relatives. Love rescues us from narrow concerns for self and those close to us, allowing us to see ourselves in others and value common goodness above division. If we have the welfare of the group in mind—helping each other, and using the resources we have wisely—we will survive. But if self-interest rules our relationships and our attitude toward our journey, our species' chances of survival are diminished.

Love not only connects us to the whole human family and secondarily to all life, it is our umbilical cord to the source of life from which we came and to which we return. It can enhance the quality and depth of life beyond other powers, with no limit to its growth. At every life stage I believed I had love in its fullness, and at every stage it deepened. Now in my ninth decade, it fills me to over-flowing, mitigating physical decline and making this life era in some ways the best of all. I see people and all life with different eyes: no longer with a comparative or judicious slant, but as miracles; I see now with appreciation and connection, which has grown over a lifetime.

Spirit/Love is our lifeline to dimensions beyond us and the source of divine power in each of us.

PHOTOGRAPHY NOTES

Dedication [TOP] Robert and Ann Staffanson; [BOTTOM] Bryan Campbell, Michael Campbell, Kristin Staffanson Campbell, Cody Campbell

p.67   [TOP] open range cowboys; [BOTTOM] Robert Staffanson with Soap Creek Cattle Company rider

p.68   [TOP] Robert Staffanson

p.69   [TOP] Robert Staffanson in ranch corral; [BOTTOM] Robert and Ann Staffanson in corral

p.70   [TOP] Robert Staffanson in cattle roundup; [BOTTOM] Robert Staffanson moving roundup horses

p.71   Robert Staffanson after roundup

p.72   Robert Staffanson with Ray Krone, ranch owner

p.131   Ann Staffanson adjusting Robert's tie before concert

p.132   Robert and Ann Staffanson at Springfield Symphony Orchestra Ball

p.133   Robert Staffanson with orchestra score in Springfield Symphony Orchestra office

p.134   Robert Staffanson conducting piano concerto with Springfield Symphony Orchestra

p.135   [TOP] Robert Staffanson conducting Springfield Symphony Orchestra; [BOTTOM] Robert Staffanson checking score with Grant Johannesen, concerto pianist at rehearsal break

p.136   Robert Staffanson conferring with Springfield Symphony Orchestra musicians

p.137   [TOP] Robert Staffanson conferring with opera singers at rehearsal break; [BOTTOM] Robert and Ann Staffanson at Springfield Symphony Orchestra rehearsal break

p.138   Robert Staffanson rehearsing Springfield Symphony Chorus (only part of chorus visible)

p.140   [TOP] Julius Hereford, Princeton University Professor and Robert Staffanson's mentor and collaborator; [BOTTOM] Robert and Ann Staffanson with Arthur Fiedler, conductor of the Boston Pops Orchestra, at appearance with the Springfield Symphony Chorus

p.141   The Springfield Symphony Orchestra auditorium with sold-out attendance

p.142   Robert Staffanson in rehearsal with a mime who added his antics to Richard Strauss' *Till Eulenspiegel's Merry Pranks*

p.143   *Till Eulenspiegel* mime with French Horn player

p.144   [TOP] Robert Staffanson with Gloria Davey, soprano, listening to orchestra playback for FM broadcast; [BOTTOM] Ann serving coffee to orchestra players at rehearsal intermission

p.145   [TOP] Robert Staffanson with Leonard Bernstein, eminent conductor, pianist, composer and writer; [BOTTOM] Robert Staffanson with Eugene Ormandy, conductor of the Philadelphia Orchestra and Robert Staffanson mentor and advocate

p.146   Robert Staffanson, Springfield Symphony Orchestra and Chorus performing in Symphony Hall

p.148   [TOP] Ann Staffanson; [BOTTOM] Ann Staffanson "Golden Girl" model for Breck Company Hair Products

p.149   Robert Staffanson conducting

p.230   Crow riders

p.231   Crow riders

p.232   Traditional Elders Circle encampment with Spanish Peaks Wilderness in background

*p.*234   [TOP] Traditional Elders Circle members at 25th Anniversary encampment, 2002; [BOTTOM] center figure with feather headdress - Donna Maria Meshoulan, Azteca, from Mexico

*p.*235   [TOP] Oren Lyons, Onondaga, speaking in the first Traditional Elders Circle encampment at the Missouri River Headwaters in Montana, 1977; [BOTTOM] Oren Lyons speaking at the 25th Anniversary of Traditional Elders Circle, 2002

*p.*236   Oren Lyons, Onondaga - 2002 Elders Circle 25th Anniversary

*p.*237   [TOP LEFT] Gileel Angaangaq - Eskimo; [TOP RIGHT] Harry Beauchamp, Assiniboine in Elders Circle council camp; [BOTTOM] Salish/Flathead drum group at council camp

*p.*238   Traditional Elders Circle council camp at twilight

*p.*240   Joe Medicine Crow, Crow, oldest member of the Traditional Elders Circle, age 104

*p.*241   [TOP] Gileel Angaangaq, Eskimo in sealskin dress with sealskin drum and Betty Laverdure, Chippewa, members of the Elders Circle; [BOTTOM] Assinitoine and Pima children

*p.*242   [TOP] Robert Staffanson with his family receiving a gift at the 25th anniversary of the Traditional Elders Circle, 2002; [BOTTOM] tipis at Traditional Elders circle encampment

INDEX

A

Abert, Grant, 185
Accra, 115–116
Alberta, 157–158
Albom, Mitch, xv
American Fur Company, 32
American Indian Institute, xv, 174–175, 180–181, 187
American Indian Law Alliance, 190
American Indian Movement (AIM), 177
Anderson, Marian, 126
Angaangaq, Gileel, *237, 241*
Antagonists, 214
Apartheid, 207, 212, 215–216
Apologists, 214
Arthur Judson Management, 101–102
Assiniboine, 50, 127, 128
Astor, John Jacob, 32

B

Babcock, Tim, 185
Bad Wound, Louie, 192
Barzin, Leon, 111–112, 114
Baucus, Max, 213
Bayacya, Thomas, 220
BBC Symphony Orchestra, 117–118
Beauchamp, Harry, *237*
Bernstein, Leonard, 103, *145*
Berry, Wendell, xiv, 121–122
Big Hole Battlefield, 49–50
Big Sky, 174
Billings school system, 76–78
Billings Symphony, 78–79
Blackfoot, 18–19, 158, 161, 224

Blixen, Karen Dinesen, 192, 214–215
Blood Indians, xii, 18–19, 124, 128, 154, 157, 159, 161, 168
Bodmer, Karl, 130
Boston Pops Orchestra, 102, *140*
Bovetti, Keith, 224
Breck, Edward, 83, 106, 109, 120
Breck, Gertrude, 109
Bronne, Arianna, 107
Brothers Circle, 189
Browning, Steve, 213
Brundtland, Gro Harlem, 219
Buffalo Bill Historic Center, 171
Buffalo jump, 178
Bundle transfer ceremony, 164–166
Bureau of Indian Affairs, 153, 176, 186
Buthelezi, Mangosuthu, 211

C

Canada, 129, 154, 157
Canoy, Bill, 38–39
Caregivers, 43–44
Carl Seashore test, 76
Catlin, George, 130
Campbell, Bryan, *Dedication*, 172
Campbell, Cody, *Dedication*, 34-35, 172
Campbell, Kristin (Staffanson), *Dedication*, v, 171-173
Campbell, Michael, v, 172
Childhood, 35–36

Children, 27, 128, 201–202
Chippewa, iv
Chippewa-Cree, 127
Chomsky, Noam, 151, 159
Civil War, 128, 129
Conducting, 124–125
Copland, Aaron, 103–104
Cowboys, 23–66
Cree, 187, 192, 193
Crow, iii, 127, 180, *230, 231*
Crowder, John, 102
Crow Fair, 155
Custer, George Armstrong, 29
"Custer Battlefield," 156

D
Dances, 59–60
Davey, Gloria, *144*
Deer, Phillip, 180, 187
Dependency, 244
Dine, 171–172
Dinesen, Isak, 214–215
Dockstader, Fred, 222
Do-gooders, 214
Downs, Olin, 74

E
Eames, Charles, 178
Education, 61–63, 201–202
Elders Circle, 188, 189, 190–191, 193–194, 198, 202–204, 221, 232, 234, *235, 237, 238, 240, 241, 242*
Endich, Sara Mae, 95
Erickson, John R., 23

F
Fantasia (film), 74
Fiedler, Arthur, 87, 102–103
Fishing, 52
Flathead, 50, 127
Flooding, 30–31

Flu pandemic, 44
Flying D Ranch, 196
Fort Union, 32–33
Frichner, Tonya Gonnela, 190

G
Gallagher, Mike, 77
Gedda, Nicholai, 92, 95
Ghana, 115–116
Goodman, Benny, 58
Gorbachev, Mikhail, 221
Grant, John, 48
Great Depression, 45
Gros Ventre, 127

H
Haidas, 220
Headwaters, 178–180, 182, 185, *235*
Heifetz, Jascha, 99–100
Hereford, Julius, 85–87, *140*
Hoffman, E. T. A., 73
Holocaust, 159
Hopi, ii, iii, 152, 179, 187, 218
Horseback riding, 23–27, 39–40
Hunting, 51–52
Huntley, Chet, 174

I
Iroquois, xii, 181, 187, 193, 218

J
James, Will, 55
Jaye, Meri, 185
Johannesen, Grant, *135*
Johnson Foundation, 177–178

K
Kamber, Chip, 208–210
Keel, Howard, 123

Kikuyu, 192
King, Martin Luther, Jr., 156–157
Kiva New, Lloyd, 175–176
Kohrs, Conrad, 48–49
Krone, Ray, *72*

L

Language, 123, 245
LaRoque, Lester, 30, 128
Laverdure, Betty, *241*
Lehman, Lotte, 125–126
Lewis and Clark, 41, 152
Liberation, 216–217
Life partners, 170
Little Missouri National Grassland, 17–18, 41
Locklin, Bill, 177
London, 116–119, 161–162
Long Tree Creek, 30
Love, 248–249
Lucero, José, xiv, 196–197, 201
Lupot, Nicolas, 57
Lyons, Oren, *i*, i–v, xii, xiii, 178, 179, 180, 182, 204, 205, 211, 217, 220, *235, 236*

M

Maasai, 192
Manifest destiny, 153
Mansfield, Mike, 223–224
Marriage, 64
Martin, Vance, 205
McDowell, Joe, 185
McLellan saddles, 208
McNickle, D'Arcy, 175
Medicine bundles, 165–166
Medicine Crow, Joe, v, 196, *240*
Meshoulan, Donna Maria, *234*
Milk River, 41–42

Millennials, 17
Miller, Glen, 58
Miller, Margot, 185
Milliken, Roger, 185
Minneapolis Symphony, 102
Missouri Headwaters, 178–180, 182, 185, *235*
Mohawk, iii
Mohawk Trail, 88
Montana, 155–156
Montana State Prison, 57
Moral education, 35–36
Mount Holyoke College, 87–88, 98–99
Moyers, Bill, 181
Music, 58–59, 61, 73–130, 154, 245–247
Muskogee, iii, 180

N

Navajo, v, 99, 171–172
New York Philharmonic, 87
Nez Perce, 49, 156
Nikolaidi, Elena, 93–94
Nkrumah, Kwame, 116
Northern Cheyenne, iii, 127
Ntombela, Magqubu, 204, 206–207, 215

O

O'Connor, George, 183–184, 185
Oglala Sioux, 192
Old Coyote, Barney, 175, 176
Oneida, 222
Onondaga, iii, v, xii, 179, 181, 187, 219
Open minds, 214
Opera, 93–96
Ormandy, Eugene, x, x–xi, 18, 74–75, 78–79, 80–81, 83, 85, 102, 123, *145*

Ortiz, Alfonso, 175, 178

P
Paris, 111–114
Partnership, 170
Paul Winter "Consort," 105
Phi Delta Theta fraternity, 63
Philadelphia Orchestra, 18, 73–76, 79–81, 102, 123
Piegan Blackfoot, 127, 157
Pima, 201–202
Pishkun, 178
Plains Indians, 27, 127, 164
Player, Ian, 207
Paramananda, Swami, 221
Pratt, Richard H., 201
Pryce, Leontyne, 126
Puyallup, iii

R
Race, 32
Racine, Abe, 50–51
Ralston, J. K., 33
Ranch life, 120–121
Red Crow, Frank, 160, 164
Red Lake Chippewa, iv
Roberts, Ann, 185
Romanticists, 214
Rosenthal, Don, 100
Rosenthal, Paul, 99–101
Rural landscape, 29–30
Russell, Charles, 42
Ryan, Tom, 54–55

S
Sacajawea, 152
Saddles, 208
Salish, 50, 127, 175
Santa Clara Pueblo, xiv, 201
Sapa Dawn Center, 203
Sargent, Malcolm, 117–118
Schwartz, Morrie, xv

Science, 199–200
Seneca, iii
Shaw, Artie, 58
Shenandoah, Audrey, 219–220
Shenandoah, Leon, 193, 220
Shoshone, 152
Singing, 92
Sioux, 42, 192
Six Nations Iroquois Confederacy, xii, 181, 187
Smith, Frankie Ann, 64, 109–110
Snake, Reuben, 226
South Africa, 204–205, 208, 211–212
Spanish, Nora, 127–128, 157
Spanish, Willie, 128, 157, 160–161, 166
Spanish flu, 44
Spirit, 243–244, 248
Spirituality, 151
Springfield Massachusetts Symphony, 58, 81–85, 96–97, 101–102, 106–107, *132, 134, 135, 137, 141, 146*
Staffanson, (Frankie) Ann, *Dedication* xi, xii, 64, 65, 69, 73, 74, 88, 89, 96-98, 109-110, 115, 119-120, 127, 129, 131, 132, 137, 140, 148, 155, 167-168, 170-173, 185
Staffanson, Kristin, *Dedication*, v, 171-173
Starker, Janos, 108
Stokowski, Leopold, 74, 102
Stravinsky, Igor, 105–106
Supernatural, 166–167

T

Tewa, 175, 196

Threshold Foundation, 185

Time, 17–21

Toscanini, Arturo, 98, 126

Traditional Circle of Indian Elders and Youth, iii, xii–xiii, 182, 204, 219, 225, *232*

Trapping, 51–52

Treigle, Norman, 92, 95

Turner, Ted, xiv, 196

Two Circles, iii–iv, v, 172, 179, 180–181, 184, 185, 188, 200–201, 216, 217–218, 226–227

U

Unity Caravan, ii, 187

Universal language, 245

University of Montana, 61–63, 65

V

Vaughan Williams, Ralph, 117, 118

Verity, William, Jr., 224–225

Violin, 57–58, 91–92

Vittachi, Tarzie, 221

Vocals, 61, 92

W

Wannabees, 214

Warfield, William, 126

Water, 169

We Are the Peoples of the Earth, 220–221

Weasel Head, Pat, 160, 161, 162, 164, 165

West, 29–30

Western Massachusetts Young People's Symphony, 83, 96, 97–98

White Shell Girl, 171–172

Wilderness Leadership School, 205–209

Wildness, 31

Wilkinson, Todd, ix–xvi

Williams, Emlyn, 118, 162

"Wingspread," 177–178

Winnebago, 226

Winter, Paul, 104–105

Women, 43–44

World War II, 85–86

Wounded Knee, 29, 177

Wright, Frank Lloyd, 177–178

Y

Yellowstone River, 26, 28, 30

Yellowtail, Tom, 180, 203–204

Yomiuri Shimbun, 222–223

Z

Zulu, 204, 206

CPSIA information can be obtained
at www.ICGtesting.com
Printed in the USA
BVHW091139191220
595946BV00001B/4

9 781942 545217